BEST 핵심 문법 총망라!

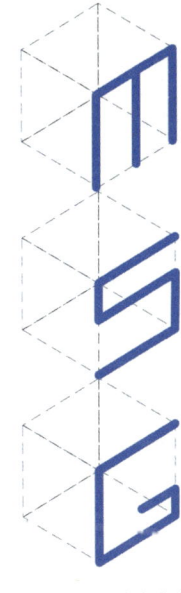

대학편입·공무원·수능·공인영어 대비
My Smart Grammar

김영편입
컨텐츠평가연구소
편저

김영편입

 대학편입, 공무원, 수능, 공인영어시험 등에서 실시하는 대부분의 영어 시험에서 문법 문제의 비중이 과거에 비해 줄어든 것은 주지의 사실입니다. 그러나 여러 내적, 외적 요인들로 초래된 경쟁의 심화로 인해 문법 문제가 갖는 실질적인 비중과 중요성이 크게 줄어들지 않은 것 또한 부인할 수 없습니다. 즉, 영어시험의 중심이 독해로 옮겨가긴 했으나, 고득점을 위해서 꼭 잡아야 할 영역은 문법입니다. 한편으로 다행스러운 것은 대부분의 영어시험에서 출제되고 있는 문법 문제는 그 범위가 한정되어 있어서, 빈출되는 핵심 문법 사항을 반복해서 학습하고 정리할 수 있다면 독해를 중심으로 시험 준비를 하면서 문법에서도 좋은 점수를 올리는 것이 가능합니다.

My Smart Grammar

My Smart Grammar는 이와 같은 배경에서 나오게 된 책입니다. My Smart Grammar는 전반적인 문법 학습을 마친 수험생들이 스마트하게 문법을 정리, 암기하고, 문제를 푸는 과정에서 궁금하거나 확인이 필요한 문법 사항들을 빠르게 찾아볼 수 있도록 했습니다. My Smart Grammar에는 대부분의 영어시험에서 출제되는 모든 문법 사항이 빠짐없이 수록돼 있으므로, 책의 내용을 벗어나는 문제는 거의 없을 것이라 확신합니다. 또한 휴대하기 편한 사이즈로 제작하여 언제 어디서든 틈틈이 반복 학습을 할 수 있도록 한 것도 큰 장점입니다.

시험장에 들어가는 순간까지 My Smart Grammar를 손에서 놓지 않고 반복해서 읽으면, 어느 순간 방대한 문법 사항이 저절로 머리에 남아 있게 될 것입니다. 모쪼록 My Smart Grammar가 수험생 여러분의 문법 실력을 향상하는 데 큰 도움이 되길 바랍니다.

김영편입 영어컨텐츠연구팀

Contents

007	제1강 동사(Verb)
043	제2강 시제(Tense)
055	제3강 수동태(Passive Voice)
069	제4강 가정법(Subjunctive Mood)
077	제5강 조동사(Auxiliary Verb)
085	제6강 부정사(Infinitive)
097	제7강 동명사(Gerund)
105	제8강 분사(Participle)
119	제9강 접속사(Conjunction)
135	제10강 관계사(Relative)
147	제11강 명사와 관사(Noun & Article)
167	제12강 대명사(Pronoun)
179	제13강 형용사(Adjective)
191	제14강 부사(Adverb)
199	제15강 비교(Comparison)
211	제16강 일치(Agreement)
217	제17강 병치(Parallelism)
221	제18강 도치(Inversion)
225	제19강 전치사(Preposition)
233	제20강 특수구문(Particular Sentence)

동사(Verb)

1. 문장의 5형식

1) 1형식 (S + V): 완전자동사

Time **flies**.

2) 2형식 (S + V + C): 불완전자동사

This **is** a great book.

3) 3형식 (S + V + O): 완전타동사

He **likes** robots.

4) 4형식 (S + V + I.O + D.O): 수여동사

She **gave** me a watch.

5) 5형식 (S + V + O + O.C): 불완전타동사

They **made** us happy.

2. 의미에 유의해야 할 완전자동사

타동사로 쓰이는 때와 매우 다른 의미를 가진다.

1) count, matter 중요하다(= be important)

> His opinion does not **count**.
> Your age does not **matter** to me.

2) do 족하다, 충분하다(= be enough)

> Any book **will do**, if it is interesting. <조동사 will 반드시 동반>

3) pay 수지가 맞다, 이익이 되다(= be profitable)

> Farming doesn't **pay** these days.

4) work 작동하다(= operate); 효과가 있다(= be effective)

> The computer still doesn't **work**.
> The pills the doctor gave me aren't **working**.

3. 수동의 의미를 지닌 자동사

능동형으로 수동의 의미를 나타내는 자동사들로, 부사와 함께 쓰이며 일반적인 경향을 나타낸다.

> This novel **sells** well. <팔리다>
> This pen **writes** well. <써지다>
> This knife **cuts** well. <잘리다>
> This car **drives** well. <운전이 되다>
> This book **reads** easily. <읽히다>
> This sweater **washes** well. <세탁이 되다>
> This glass **breaks** easily. <깨지다>

4. 불완전자동사

1) 보어의 형태

불완전자동사는 주어의 동작이나 상태를 보충하는 보어를 필요로 한다. 보어로는 명사(상당어구)나 형용사(상당어구)가 올 수 있다.

> She **became** *a figure skater*. <명사 보어, 주어와 동격>
> She **seems** *mature* for her age. <형용사 보어, 주어의 상태 설명>
> The human body **is** *like a complex machine*. <전치사 + 명사>
> He **seems** *to have no friend besides you*. <부정사구>
> His hobby **is** *collecting stamps*. <동명사구>
> The game **grew** *exciting* as time went by. <현재분사>
> We **get** *excited* when we think about going on a trip. <과거분사>
> A bigger problem **is** *that people waste so much water*. <명사절>

2) 상태의 유지·지속을 나타내는 불완전자동사

continue, hold, keep, lie, remain, stand, stay 등

> She may stay here so long as she **keeps** *quiet*.
> I'm afraid that I may **remain** *single* for life.
> Our offer **holds** *good* until the end of this year.
> We will **stand** *firm* against a worldwide terrorism network.

3) 상태의 변화를 나타내는 불완전자동사

become, come, fall, get, go, grow, run, turn 등

> He **became** *healthier* than he was last year.
> After you **fall** *asleep*, your muscles relax.
> As she **grew** *older*, her eyes **became** *dim*.
> He's not so bad once you **get** *to know* him.

(cf.) come, get, grow의 경우에는 to부정사를 보어로 취할 수 있지만, '~이 되다'라는 뜻으로 쓰이는 become 뒤에는 to부정사가 올 수 없음에 유의한다.
As we grow older, we **become** **to know* the limit of our ability. (×)
As we grow older, we **come** *to know* the limit of our ability. (○)

4) 감각을 나타내는 불완전자동사

look, sound, feel, smell, taste + 형용사
look, sound, feel, smell, taste + like + 명사

I always **feel** *tired* after I work out.
Appetizing food always **smells** *delicious*.
That melody **sounds** *familiar* for some reason.
You're trying to be cool but you **look like** *a fool* to me.

(cf.) 보어 자리에 부사를 쓰지 않도록 특히 유의해야 한다.
She **looked** **beautifully* in the dress. (×)
She **looked** *beautiful* in the dress. (○)

5) 입증·판명을 나타내는 불완전자동사

come out, prove, turn out 등

To my surprise, he **proved** (to be) *an arsonist*.
His prediction **turned out** (to be) *correct*.
That story **came out** (to be) *true*.

6) 판단을 나타내는 불완전자동사

appear, seem 등

He **appeared** (to be) *an honest person* to me.
= It appeared that he was an honest person to me.
They **seem** *to know* a lot about James Bond.
= It seems that they know a lot about James Bond.

5. 준보어(유사보어)

1형식 문장에 쓰인 완전자동사 다음에 쓰여 추가적으로 주어의 상태나 동작을 나타내는 보어를 뜻한다. 문장의 구성에 필수적인 요소는 아니므로, 준보어가 없어도 문장은 성립한다.

He **died** *rich*.
= When he died, he was rich.
All men **are created** *equal*.
She **lay** *smiling* at me.

(cf.) My daughter **returned** home *safe*. 〈safe: 준보어 – 돌아왔을 때의 상태〉
  My daughter **returned** home *safely*. 〈safely: 부사 – 돌아온 방법〉
(cf.) 타동사 뒤에 준보어가 쓰이는 경우에는 목적어의 상태를 나타낸다.
  We prefer to **eat** fish *raw* here, as the Japanese do.

6. 자동사 + 전치사

자동사가 전치사와 함께 동사구를 이루면 타동사처럼 목적어를 가질 수 있다.

1) abstain from ~을 삼가다

> He **abstained from** eating for six days.

2) account for ~을 설명하다; ~을 차지하다; ~의 원인이다

> How do you **account for** the show's success?
> The Japanese market **accounts for** 35% of the company's revenue.
> The poor weather may have **accounted for** the small crowd.

3) concentrate on ~에 집중하다

> I couldn't **concentrate on** the movie.

4) consist in ~에 있다(= lie in)
   consist of ~로 이루어져 있다(= be composed of, be made up of)

> Happiness **consists in** contentment.
> The committee **consists of** ten members.

5) graduate from ~를 졸업하다

> Miranda will **graduate from** college soon.

6) insist on ~을 주장하다

> We **insisted on** a refund of the full amount.

7) participate in ~에 참가하다

> Everybody **participated in** a riot.

8) resort to ~에 의존하다

> They felt obliged to **resort to** violence.

9) wait for ~을 기다리다
   wait on ~을 시중들다

> Jason **waited for** his girlfriend for an hour.
> She **waits on** customers all day at the restaurant.

10) agree to + 사물 ~에 동의하다
    agree with + 사람 ~와 의견이 맞다

> We cannot **agree to** such a proposal.
> I cannot **agree with** you on the matter.

11) amount to (총계·금액이) ~이 되다; 결국 ~이 되다

> The annual net profit **amounts to** ten million dollars.
> Her answer **amounted to** a complete refusal.

12) apologize to A for B A에게 B를 사과하다

> I must **apologize to** you **for** not writing for such a long time.

13) succeed in ~에 성공하다, 번창하다
    succeed to ~을 상속[계승]하다

> He **succeeded in** solving the problem.
> He **succeeded to** his father's estate.

(cf.) succeed ~의 뒤를 잇다

> He **succeeded** his father as the owner of the estate.

14) belong to ~에 속하다, ~의 소유이다

The blue coat **belongs to** her.

15) complain of[about] ~에 대해 불평하다

She **complained of** the room being dirty.

16) conform to ~에 따르다, 순응하다

He refused to **conform to** the local customs.

17) deal with ~을 다루다, 처리하다
deal in ~을 거래하다, 장사하다

Her poems often **deal with** the subject of death.
The merchant **deals in** wool and cotton.

18) depend on[upon] ~에 달려 있다; ~에 의지하다

His success **depends on** effort and ability.
He **depended on** his uncle for school expenses.

19) dispense with ~없이 지내다(= do without); ~을 필요 없게 하다

We cannot **dispense with** the necessities of life.
Credit cards **dispense with** the need for cash altogether.

20) dispose of ~을 처분[양도]하다, 버리다

It's very difficult to **dispose of** nuclear waste.

21) interfere with ~을 방해하다
interfere in ~을 간섭하다

Don't **interfere with** him while he's working.
You should not **interfere in** another's life.

22) laugh at ~을 비웃다

> Never **laugh at** your friends' personal choices such as clothes and shoes.

23) object to ~에 반대하다, 항의하다

> Many local people **object to** the building of the new airport.

24) result from ~에서 기인하다
result in ~을 초래하다, ~의 결과로 되다, 귀착하다

> Disease often **results from** poverty.
> His efforts **resulted in** failure.

25) arrive at[in] ~에 도착하다

> The train **arrived at** the station 20 minutes late.

26) cooperate with ~와 협력하다, 협동하다

> The two groups agreed to **cooperate with** each other.

27) compete with ~와 경쟁하다, 겨루다

> There is no book that can **compete with** this.

28) experiment with ~을 실험하다

> He **experimented with** electromagnetic waves.

29) coincide with ~와 일치하다(= correspond to); ~와 동시에 일어나다

> Your views exactly **coincide with** mine.
> The two events **coincided with** each other.

30) sympathize with ~에 공감하다; ~을 동정하다

> I **sympathize with** what you would like to do.
> I **sympathize with** her in her suffering.

7. 자동사로 혼동하기 쉬운 타동사

우리말 해석이 주는 느낌과는 달리, 타동사이므로 뒤에 전치사가 쓰이지 못한다.

1) accompany ~에 동반하다; (현상 따위가) ~에 수반하여 일어나다

> His wife **accompanied** ~~with~~ him on the trip.
> Wind **accompanied** ~~with~~ the rain.

2) affect ~에 영향을 미치다

> His laziness will truly **affect** ~~on~~ his school grades.

3) address ~에게 말을 걸다; ~에게 연설[인사]하다; ~을 역점을 두어 다루다

> A stranger **addressed** ~~to~~ us in Spanish.
> He **addressed** ~~to~~ an assembly.
> They **addressed** ~~with~~ the plan seriously.

4) approach ~에 접근하다, 다가가다

> A lady **approached** ~~to~~ me to ask the way to the station.

5) attend ~에 출석하다, 참석하다

> I have to **attend** ~~at~~ the meeting now.

(cf.) attend to ~에 주의하다/ attend on ~을 시중들다, 간호하다
   Attend to what your teacher says.
   The nurses **attended on** the sick day and night.

6) await ~을 기다리다(= wait for)

   We must **await for** his decision.

7) answer ~에게 대답하다(= reply to)

   Have you **answered to** her letter?

   (cf.) answer for ~에 대해 책임지다
   You have to **answer for** your behavior.

8) become ~와 어울리다

   The new shirt **becomes to** you.

9) call ~에게 전화하다

   My brother **called to** me from Spain last night.

10) comprise ~로 구성되어 있다(= consist of)

    The United States of America **comprises of** 50 states.

11) contact ~와 접촉하다, 연락하다

    Please **contact with** me when you come to Korea again.

12) discuss ~에 관해 토론하다

    I'd like to **discuss about** the delivery schedules.

13) enter ~에 들어가다

    Someone **entered into** the room behind me.

    (cf.) enter into ~을 시작하다, 개시하다
    He **entered into** the business.

14) greet ~에게 인사하다

He **greeted** ~~to~~ all the guests warmly as they arrived.

15) inhabit ~에서 살다, 거주하다(= live in)

The animal **inhabits** ~~in~~ dry grassland.

16) marry ~와 결혼하다

When I **marry** ~~with~~ her, I'll build a nice house.

17) mention ~에 대해 언급하다

Did she **mention** ~~about~~ where she was going?

18) obey ~에 복종하다, 따르다

The driver didn't **obey** ~~to~~ the traffic laws.

19) oppose ~에 반대하다, 이의를 제기하다(= object to)

We all **opposed** ~~to~~ his suggestion.

20) reach ~에 도착하다(= arrive at)

They **reached** ~~at~~ the station on time.

21) resemble ~와 닮다(= take after)

The boy **resembles** ~~with~~ his father closely.

22) survive ~에서 생존하다[살아남다]; (남보다) 오래 살다

The crew **survived** ~~from~~ the shipwreck.
He **survived** ~~from~~ his children by a few years.

제1강 동사

23) match ~에 어울리다

The doors were painted blue to **match** ~~with~~ the walls.

24) follow ~을 쫓다, 따라가다

The dog **followed** ~~after~~ me to the house.

(cf.) suffer + 패배, 손실, 모욕
suffer from + 질병, 가난, 기아
He **suffered** *the capital punishment* for his murder.
He **suffered from** *mental illness.*

8. to부정사를 목적어로 취하는 동사

1) want, would like, hope, wish, desire, care 원하다, 기대하다, 바라다

I **want** *to leave* this city.

2) expect 기대하다, 예상하다

You can't **expect** *to learn* a foreign language in a few months.

3) decide, determine, resolve, choose 결정하다, 결심하다

He **decided** *to start* his own business.

4) plan, mean 계획하다, 의도하다

We are **planning** *to visit* Europe this winter.
I didn't **mean** *to hurt* your feeling.

(cf.) Punctuality **means** *being* on time. ('의미하다'의 뜻으로 쓰임)

5) promise 약속하다

The college principal **promised** *to look into* the matter.

6) agree, consent 동의하다

They **agreed** *to accept* the offer.

7) offer 제안하다, 제의하다

He **offered** *to accompany* her.

8) refuse 거절하다

He **refused** *to admit* his fault.

9) pretend, affect ~인 체하다, 가장하다

She **pretended** *not to know* me.

10) afford ~할 여유가 있다, ~할 수 있다 <조동사 can을 수반>

We **cannot afford** *to keep* the luxurious car.

11) manage 이럭저럭 해내다, 간신히 ~하다

I **managed** *to get* there in time.

12) need 필요하다

He **needs** *to learn* English.

13) seek, strive, struggle, endeavor 애쓰다, 노력하다

The rabbit **struggled** *to escape* from the snare.

14) ask, beg, demand 요구하다, 부탁하다

The man **asked** *to come* with us.

제1강 동사

15) fail ~을 (하지) 못하다

> She **failed** *to get* into art college.

(cf.) never fail to 반드시 ~하다(= be sure to)
> She **never fails to** email every week.

16) hesitate 망설이다, 주저하다

> She **hesitated** *to take* his offer.

17) tend ~하는 경향이 있다

> Women **tend** *to live* longer than men.

18) threaten 위협하다

> The hijackers **threatened** *to kill* one passenger every hour.

19) claim 주장하다

> He **claimed** *to have reached* the top of the mountain.

20) long 열망하다, 동경하다

> I'm **longing** *to see* you again.

9. 동명사를 목적어로 취하는 동사

1) enjoy 즐기다

> She **enjoys** *watching* movies.

2) finish, quit, give up, abandon, stop 끝내다, 그만두다, 중단하다

He **stopped** *smoking*.

(cf.) stop + to부정사 ~하기 위해 멈추다
He **stopped** *to smoke*.

3) suggest, advise, recommend, advocate 제안하다, 권유하다, 주장하다

Father **suggested** *going* on a picnic.

4) avoid, escape, evade, mind, resist 회피하다, 꺼리다

He narrowly **escaped** *being* killed.

5) postpone, put off, defer, delay 연기하다, 지연하다

The couple had to **postpone** *purchasing* a car.

6) admit, allow, acknowledge, permit 인정하다, 허락하다

He **admitted** *having stolen* the money.

7) anticipate 기대하다

He **anticipated** *getting* a letter from his uncle in England.

8) practice 연습하다

My son **practices** *playing* the piano every day.

9) dislike 싫어하다

Though she **disliked** *going* to funerals, she knew she had to be there.

10) deny 부인하다

The accused man **denies** *meeting* her.

제1강 동사

11) forbid 금지하다

　　The police **forbade** *entering* the house.

12) appreciate 감사하다

　　I would **appreciate** *receiving* a copy of the book.

13) consider, contemplate 숙고하다

　　I am **considering** *buying* a new car.

14) imagine, fancy 상상하다

　　I couldn't **imagine** *meeting* you here.

15) include, involve 포함하다

　　Your duties **include** *typing* letters and *answering* the telephone.

16) resent 분개하다

　　I **resent** his *being* too arrogant.

17) miss ~하지 못하다, ~하는 것을 놓치다

　　We **missed** *seeing* that film.

18) risk 감히 ~하다, ~하는 위험을 무릅쓰다

　　I'm willing to **risk** *losing* everything.

19) recall 상기하다

　　I can't **recall** *meeting* her before.

20) **favor** 찬성하다, 지지하다

> I **favored** *traveling* by night when the road was quiet.

10. to부정사와 동명사 모두를 목적어로 취하는 동사

1) 의미의 차이가 없는 경우

attempt, begin, cease, continue, intend, start 등

> They **ceased** *to give*[*giving*] money to charity.
> Scientists **continued** *to debate*[*debating*] the history of man.
> She **intends** *to sell*[*selling*] her home.
> My grandmother **began** *to tell*[*telling*] a tale.

(cf.) begin, start는 진행시제인 경우와 know, understand, realize 등이 오는 경우에는 to부정사를 목적어로 쓴다.
> It **was starting** *to rain*.
> I slowly **began** *to understand* how she felt.

2) 의미의 차이가 있는 경우

① try + to부정사 ~하려고 애쓰다, 노력하다
   try + 동명사 시험 삼아 ~을 해보다

> I **tried** *to exercise* in the gym every day.
> They **tried** *climbing* the tree.

② like, love, prefer, hate + to부정사 구체적인 경향이나 일시적 사실
   like, love, prefer, hate + 동명사 일반적인 경향이나 습관

> I don't **like** *to drink*. <지금 술을 마시고 싶지 않다.>
> I don't **like** *drinking*. <평소에도 술을 좋아하지 않는다.>

③ be sure[certain] + to부정사 ~할 것임에 틀림없다
　 be sure[certain] + of + 동명사 ~할 것임을 확신하다

> Tom **is sure** *to pass* the test. <합격의 주체는 Tom, 확신의 주체는 I>
> Tom **is sure of** *passing* the test. <합격의 주체와 확신의 주체가 모두 Tom>

④ go on + 동명사 하던 일을 계속하다
　 go on + to부정사 어떤 일이 끝나고 이어서 다른 일을 계속하다

> He **went on** *talking* for hours, and it drove me crazy.
> After talking about his friend, he **went on** *to talk* about his money matter.

3) 시제 차이가 있는 경우

remember, forget, regret + to부정사 <미래의 일>
remember, forget, regret + 동명사 <과거의 일>

> I **remember** *to meet* you tomorrow.
> I **remember** *meeting* you yesterday.
> I **forgot** *to bring* my umbrella with me.
> I **forgot** *putting* my bag in my drawer.
> I **regret** *to say* that I am unable to help you. <유감>
> I **regret** *buying* that new copy machine. <후회>

11. 목적어 뒤에 전치사를 취하는 동사

1) 공급동사 + A + with + B

provide[supply/ furnish] A with B　A에게 B를 공급하다, 제공하다
charge A with B　A에게 B의 임무[책임]를 지우다; A를 B에 대해 고발하다
endow A with B　A에게 B를 주다, 부여하다
entrust A with B　A에게 B를 맡기다
equip A with B　A에 B를 장비시키다, 갖추게 하다
present A with B　A에게 B를 증정하다, 바치다

> We **provide** the children **with** food.
> = We **provide** food **for** the children.
> They **supply** us **with** oil.
> = They **supply** oil **to** us.
> He **furnished** the hungry **with** food.
> = He **furnished** food **to** the hungry.
> The police **charged** him **with** theft.
> Nature has **endowed** him **with** great ability.

2) 금지동사 + 목적어 + from ~ing

prevent[keep/ discourage/ stop/ prohibit/ deter/ dissuade/ bar/ hinder] + A + from ~ing A로 하여금 ~하지 못하게 하다

> His wife **prevented** him **from going** abroad.
> The rain **kept** us **from playing** soccer.
> Who can **stop** her **from behaving** like that?

(cf.) forbid + 목적어 + to부정사
　　Laws **forbids** minors **to smoke**.
　　Laws **forbids** minors **from smoking**. (△)

3) 제거/박탈동사 + A + of + B

rob[deprive/ strip] A of B A에게서 B를 빼앗다, 박탈하다
rid A of B A에서 B를 제거하다
relieve[ease] A of B A에게서 B를 덜어주다
cure[heal] A of B A에게서 B를 고치다
clear A of B A에서 B를 치우다, 제거하다

> A highwayman **robbed** the traveler **of** his money.
> The dictatorship **deprived** people **of** their freedom.
> We must **rid** the house **of** rats.
> The doctor **relieved** his patient **of** headache.

(cf.) rob + 사람/장소 + of + 사물
　　steal + 사물 + from + 사람/장소
　　The boys **robbed** her **of** the smartphone.
　　The boys **stole** the smartphone **from** her.

제1강 동사

4) 통고/확신/고발/설득동사 + A + of + B

remind A of B A에게 B를 상기시키다
inform[notify] A of B A에게 B를 알리다, 통보하다
convince[assure] A of B A에게 B를 확신시키다
accuse A of B A를 B로 고발하다; 비난하다
persuade A of B A에게 B를 설득하다
convict A of B A에게 B의 판결을 내리다
suspect A of B A에게 B의 혐의를 두다
warn A of B A에게 B를 경고하다

> You **remind** me **of** your father.
> She **informed** her parents **of** her safe arrival.
> He **convinced** me **of** his innocence.
> His wife **accused** him **of** adultery.
> The jury **convicted** him **of** forgery.

5) 상벌동사 + A + for + B

blame[criticize/ reprimand] A for B A를 B때문에 비난하다
scold A for B A를 B때문에 꾸짖다
punish A for B A를 B때문에 벌하다
praise A for B A를 B때문에 칭찬하다
excuse A for B B에 대해서 A를 용서하다
thank A for B A에게 B를 감사하다

> They **blamed** me **for** the accident.
> = They **blamed** the accident **on** me.
> They **criticized** him **for** his bad behavior.
> They **praised** him **for** his splendid service.

6) 부가/전가의 동사 + A + to + B

attribute[ascribe/ impute] A to B A를 B의 탓으로 돌리다
add A to B A를 B에 더하다, 첨가하다
owe A to B A는 B 덕택이다

> She **attributes** her success **to** hard work and a little luck.
> He **added** sugar **to** tea.
> I **owe** everything **to** my teachers.

7) 부과/칭찬/치하의 동사 + A + on + B

   inflict A on B A를 B에게 가하다, 과하다
   impose A on B A를 B에게 부과하다
   bestow[confer] A on B A를 B에게 주다
   congratulate A on B A에게 B를 축하하다

   Judge **inflicted** the death penalty **on** the criminal.
   He **bestowed** one million dollar **on** the charity.
   We **congratulated** him **on** his success.

8) distinguish[tell/ know] A from B A를 B와 구별하다

   Speech **distinguishes** man **from** animals.

9) compare A with[to] B A를 B와 비교하다
   compare A to B A를 B에 비유하다

   We carefully **compared** the first report **with[to]** the second.
   Shakespeare **compared** the world **to** a stage.

10) mistake A for B A를 B로 잘못 보다, 착각하다

    She **mistook** sugar **for** the salt.

11) replace A with B A를 B로 대체하다, A 대신 B를 사용하다

    I **replaced** butter **with** margarine.
    = I **substituted** margarine **for** butter.

12. that절을 목적어로 취할 수 없는 동사

want, like 등은 that절을 목적어로 취할 수 없으며 5형식 문형으로 써야 한다.

I **want** *that you will come.* (×)
I **want** *you to come.* (○)

13. 수여동사

수여동사는 두 개의 목적어, 즉, '~에게'에 해당하는 간접목적어와 '~을/를'에 해당하는 직접목적어를 취하는 동사다.

> Please **give** *me* a brochure about this city.
> I will **buy** *her* a new scarf.
> They **asked** *him* several questions.
> He doesn't **envy** *others* their success.

1) 4형식 문장을 3형식 문장으로 전환하는 경우

① to를 쓰는 동사
give, show, send, hand(건네다), pass, teach, tell, bring, allow, owe, offer, do(이익·손해를 주다), award(수여하다), deny(주지 않다) 등

> I **gave** *him* a picture yesterday.
> = I **gave** a picture **to** *him* yesterday.
> She **owes** *him* a lot of money.
> = She **owes** a lot of money **to** *him*.
> Computers **do** *us* good[harm].
> = Computers **do** good[harm] **to** *us*.

② for를 쓰는 동사
buy, make, build, choose, cook, do(호의를 베풀다, 부탁을 들어주다), find, get, order(주문하다), spare(나누어주다) 등

> I **bought** *him* a photo album.
> = I **bought** a photo album **for** *him*.
> He **made** *his daughter* a box.
> = He **made** a box **for** *his daughter*.
> Could you **do** *me* a favor?
> = Could you **do** a favor **for** *me*?

③ of를 쓰는 동사
ask, inquire, require 등

> I **asked** *him* a simple question.
> = I **asked** a simple question **of** *him*.

④ 4형식에서 3형식으로 전환할 수 없는 동사 <두 목적어의 순서 전환 불가>
envy, forgive, cost, guarantee, pardon, save(덜어주다),
take(시간 등이 걸리다) 등

> He **envied** *me* my success.
> She **forgave** *me* my rudeness.
> The house **cost** *him* a great deal of money.
> Machines **save** *us* much time and trouble.

(cf.) It takes + 사람 + 시간 + to부정사
 = It takes + 시간 + for 사람 + to부정사
 It **took** *us* half an hour **to get** there by taxi.
 = It **took** half an hour for *us* **to get** there by taxi.

2) 수여동사로 오인하기 쉬운 동사

'~에게'에 해당하는 말 앞에 반드시 to가 필요하다.
explain A to B A를 B에게 설명하다
introduce A to B A를 B에게 소개하다
suggest[propose] A to B A를 B에게 제안하다
prove A to B A를 B에게 증명하다
announce A to B A를 B에게 알리다
confess A to B A를 B에게 자백하다
admit A to B A를 B에게 인정하다

> He briefly **explained** *them the situation*. (×)
> He briefly **explained** the situation **to** them. (○)
> He **introduced** *me his wife*. (×)
> He **introduced** his wife **to** me. (○)
> I **suggested** *the committee another plan*. (×)
> I **suggested** another plan **to** the committee. (○)

14. 불완전타동사

1) 목적격 보어 앞에 to be를 수반하는 동사

목적격 보어가 형용사인 경우에는 to be를 생략할 수 있다.
think, believe, suppose, find, know, feel 등

> I **believe** Jason **to be** *a good teacher*.
> = I believe that Jason is a good teacher.
> We **thought** him **(to be)** *foolish*.
> = We thought that he was foolish.

(cf.) know는 목적격 보어 앞에 항상 to be를 쓰는 것이 원칙이다.
　I **know** him **to be** *earnest*.

2) 목적격 보어 앞에 as를 수반하는 동사

목적어와 목적보어는 동격관계이며, as를 생략해서 쓸 수 없다.
regard[look upon/ think of/ view/ see] A as B A를 B로 간주하다[여기다]
refer to A as B A를 B로 부르다
describe, recognize, acknowledge A as B

> We **regard[look upon/ think of]** the dove **as** *the symbol of peace*.
> Many people **refer to** "Hamlet" **as** *Shakespeare's greatest work*.

3) 목적격 보어 앞에 to be나 as를 수반하는 동사

to be나 as를 생략할 수 있다.
consider A (as[to be]) B A를 B로 간주하다, 여기다
appoint A (as[to be]) B A를 B로 임명하다, 지정하다
elect A (as[to be]) B A를 B로 선출하다

> I **consider** him **(as [to be])** *a fool*.
> They **appointed** him **(as [to be])** *captain of the England team*.
> They **elected** him **(as[to be])** *President*.

4) 목적격 보어 앞에 to be나 as를 수반하지 않는 동사

make, call, name 등

> Jason has **made** Miranda *happy*.
> They **called** him *a liar*.
> They **named** the child *Jason*.

15. to부정사를 목적격 보어로 취하는 동사

1) advise 충고하다

> Police are **advising** people *to stay* at home.

2) allow, permit 허락하다

> My father won't **allow** me *to ride* a motorcycle.

3) ask, beg, require, request 부탁하다, 요구하다

> They **required** me *to work* harder.

4) enable ~할 수 있게 하다

> Endurance **enabled** him *to win* the race.

5) encourage 격려하다, 장려하다, 조장하다

> Banks actively **encourage** people *to borrow* money.

6) expect 기대하다, 예상하다

> I **expect** him *to pass* the exam.

7) forbid 금지하다

> Her father **forbade** her *to marry* the poor man.

8) force, compel, oblige 강요하다, 억지로 ~시키다

They **forced** him *to sign* the paper.

9) get, cause ~하도록 하다

This accident **caused** her *to change* her mind.

10) intend, mean 의도하다, ~할 작정이다

The writer **intends** his readers *to identify with* the main character.

11) lead ~할 마음이 일어나게 하다

Fear **led** him *to tell* lies.

12) leave 자유롭게 ~하게 하다, ~할 것을 허용하다

Leave her *to do* as she likes.

13) motivate ~하는 동기를 부여하다

The plans **motivate** employees *to work* more efficiently.

14) persuade, convince 설득하다, 납득시키다

I **persuaded** her *to see* a doctor.

15) teach ~하도록 가르치다

Who **taught** you *to play* the piano?

16) tell, order, command 명령하다

She **ordered** him *to leave* her room.

17) urge 재촉하다, 강하게 권하다

He **urged** her *to stay* overnight.

18) want, wish, desire 원하다, 소망하다

What do you **want** me *to do*?

16. 5형식 문형으로 쓰지 않는 주요 동사

hope, say, suggest, demand, insist 등은 5형식으로 쓰지 않고 that절을 목적어로 취한다.

I **hope** *you to come* soon. (×)
I **hope** *that you will come* soon. (○)
My family doctor **suggested** *me to take a walk* every day. (×)
My family doctor **suggested** *that I should take a walk* every day. (○)

17. 사역동사의 용법

make(강제), have(부탁, 명령), let(허락, 방임), help(도움) 등

1) make + 목적어 + 동사원형/과거분사/형용사

I'll **make** him *go* there. <목적어와 목적격 보어가 능동관계>
I could not **make** myself *understood*. <목적어와 목적격 보어가 수동관계>
Too much wine **makes** men *drunk*.

2) have + 목적어 + 동사원형/현재분사/과거분사

I **had** him *repair* my car.
He **had** us *laughing* all through the night.
I **had** my car *repaired*. <의지가 있는 경우: 시키다>
I **had** my car *stolen*. <의지가 없는 경우: 당하다>

3) let + 목적어 + 동사원형/be p.p.

> Please **let** me *know* what to do.
> **Let** the door *be opened*. <수동관계인 경우 be p.p.>

4) help + 목적어 + to부정사/동사원형

> He **helped** a lady *to get* out of the car.
> = He **helped** a lady *get* out of the car.

(cf.) help + to부정사 〈to부정사가 help의 목적어인 3형식〉
help + ~ing 〈help가 avoid의 의미〉
Go and **help** *(to) wash up* at the sink.
I could not **help** *laughing*. 나는 웃지 않을 수 없었다.

(cf.) get은 사역동사는 아니지만 사역의 의미를 갖는 동사로, 목적격 보어로 to부정사를 취한다.
get + 목적어 + to부정사
get + 목적어 + (to be) + p.p.
I **got** her *to prepare* for the party.
I am going to **get** my hair *done*. 〈시키다〉
He **got** his wrist *broken*. 〈당하다〉

18. 지각동사의 용법

see, watch, notice, observe, hear, feel, smell 등

1) 목적어와 목적격 보어의 관계가 능동이면 목적격 보어는 동사원형 또는 현재분사를 쓴다.

> I **heard** my father *call* Michael. <목적어가 call하는 행위의 주체>
> I **saw** him *crying*. <진행 중인 동작>

2) 목적어와 목적격 보어의 관계가 수동이면 목적격 보어는 과거분사를 쓴다.

> I **heard** her father *called* Michael. <목적어가 call하는 행위의 대상>

(cf.) 특정시점표시 부사어구가 있는 경우에는 목적격 보어로 현재분사만 가능하다.
I **saw** the letter **lie* on the table *this morning*. (×)
I **saw** the letter *lying* on the table *this morning*. (○)

19. 가목적어-진목적어 구문으로 쓰는 동사

believe, find, make, think, take 등

> I **make** it a rule <u>to get up early in the morning</u>.
> I **found** it difficult <u>to solve the problem</u>.
> He **made** it clear <u>that he would stay here for 5 days</u>.
> I **think** it quite natural <u>that she should get so angry</u>.
> I **took** it for granted <u>that you had read this novel</u>. <~을 당연한 것으로 여기다>

(cf.) 수식어를 동반한 명사의 경우 아무리 길더라도 가목적어 it을 쓰지 않음에 유의한다.
  The computer **made** *it possible <u>the phenomenal leap in human proficiency</u>. (×)
  The computer **made** possible <u>the phenomenal leap in human proficiency</u>. (○)

20. 기타 5형식 동사의 용법

1) keep + 목적어 + 형용사/현재분사/과거분사

> You should always **keep** your hands *clean*.
> I'm sorry to have **kept** you *waiting* so long.
> Learn to **keep** the door *shut*.

2) find + 목적어 + 형용사/현재분사/과거분사

> They **found** the book *difficult*.
> I **found** him *dozing*.
> I **found** something *stolen*.

3) get + 목적어 + 형용사/to부정사/현재분사/과거분사

> We **got** everything *ready*.
> I **got** him *to fix* my umbrella.
> He **got** the clock *going*.
> I **got** my bicycle *repaired*.

4) leave + 목적어 + 형용사/to부정사/현재분사/과거분사

> **Leave** the door *open*.
> **Leave** her *to do* as she likes.
> Don't **leave** the baby *crying*.
> Don't **leave** your homework *undone*.

5) 기타 동사

> I **caught** him *stealing* my dictionary on the desk.
> We **caught** a lion *alive*.
> Losing his fortune **drove** him *mad*.
> Hunger **drove** him *to steal*.
> They **set** slaves *free*.
> He often **sets** people *laughing*.
> The power **sets** a body *in motion*.
> The boss **set** his men *to dig* the ground.

21. 어법과 의미에 유의해야 할 기본 동사

1) lie - lay - lain ㉑ 눕다, 놓여 있다
   lay - laid - laid ㉣ ~을 눕히다, 놓다, (알을) 낳다
   lie - lied - lied ㉑ 거짓말하다

   > She just **lay** down and went straight to sleep.
   > She **laid** her hand on her son's shoulder.
   > He **lied** in order to gain the president's trust.

2) hang - hung - hung ㉣ 걸다, 매달다 ㉑ 매달리다, 드리워지다
   hang - hanged - hanged ㉣ 교수형에 처하다

   > He **hung** his hat on the hook.
   > Her hair **hung** down on her shoulders.
   > Luke was **hanged** on an olive tree in Greece.

3) rise   - rose - risen ⓐ 일어나다, (해가) 뜨다, (물가가) 오르다, 올라가다
   raise - raised - raised ⓑ 올리다, 기르다, 재배하다
   arise - arose - arisen ⓐ (사건·사고 등이) 발생하다

> The sun **rises** in the east.
> He **raised** his left hand.
> She **raised** five children.
> Accidents **arise** from carelessness.

4) sit   - sat   - sat ⓐ 앉다, 착석하다
   seat - seated - seated ⓑ 앉히다
   set   - set   - set ⓑ 두다, 놓다, 정하다

> He **sat** on the chair.
> The waiter **seated** us by the window.
> **Seat** yourself. (= Be seated. = Take your seat. = Sit down.)
> He **set** the book on the table.

5) affect - affected - affected 영향을 끼치다, 악영향을 끼치다, 작용하다
   effect - effected - effected (결과를) 초래하다, 달성하다

> This book has **affected** my thinking.
> Intemperance undoubtedly **affected** his health.
> Their continuous efforts **effected** a great change.

(cf.) The medicine had an immediate **effect**. 〈명사, 효과〉
    He realized the disastrous **effects** of war. 〈명사, 결과〉
    Overwork had an evil **effect** on his health. 〈명사, 영향〉

6) saw - sawed - sawn/ sawed 톱질하다
   sew - sewed - sewn/ sewed 꿰매다, 바느질하다
   sow - sowed - sown/ sowed 씨를 뿌리다, 퍼뜨리다

> The man **sawed** the plank into two halves.
> My mother used to **sew** a patch onto my jeans.
> The farmer **sowed** the field with rice.

제1강 동사

7) fall - fell - fallen ⓐ 떨어지다, 낙하하다, 추락하다
   fell - felled - felled ⓑ 쓰러뜨리다

   The temperature has **fallen** recently.
   He **felled** his opponent with a single blow.

8) find - found - found 발견하다, 얻다
   found - founded - founded 설립하다, 기초를 두다, 근거로 하다

   I **found** a ten-dollar bill on the floor.
   Her family **founded** the college in 1895.
   Their marriage was **founded** on love and mutual respect.
   = Their marriage was **based** on love and mutual respect.

9) bear - bore - born 낳다 <수동태에서 'by+사람'이 없는 경우>
   bear - bore - borne '낳다'의 뜻이지만 완료시제의 경우와 수동태에서 'by+사람'이 있는 경우/ '낳다'의 뜻이 아닌 경우

   He was **born** in Boston in 1972.
   My girlfriend has **borne** a child.
   The infant was **borne** *by a teenage unmarried mother*.
   She has **borne** the pain well. <'참다, 견디다'의 의미>

10) say, tell, speak

   ① say - said - said
      say + (to+ 명사) + that절
      say + 목적어

   He **said** (to his boss) that he was ill.
   She **said** nothing to him.
   Everyone **says** (that) our team will win.

   ② tell - told - told
      tell + 목적어 + to + 명사 <3형식>
      tell + 간접목적어 + 직접목적어 <4형식>
      tell + 목적어 + that절 <4형식>
      tell + 목적어 + to부정사 <5형식, 명령하다>

> He **told** the story to everybody he met.
> He **told** me the truth.
> He **told** his boss that he was ill.
> He **told** me to do that.

③ speak - spoke - spoken
　 speak + on[of/ about/ to/ with] + 명사
　 speak + 목적어(언어, 연설, 주제)

> Can I **speak** to you outside for a minute?
> How many *languages* can you **speak**?

11) wind - wound - wound ⑬ 감다 ㉂ (강·길이) 굽이치다
　　 wound - wounded - wounded ⑬ (상처를) 입히다, (부상을) 입히다

> He **wound** his watch.
> The bullet **wounded** him in the shoulder.

12) bring - brought - brought 가시고 오다, 데려오다
　　 take - took - taken 가지고 가다, 데려가다
　　 fetch - fetched - fetched (가서) 가져오다, 데리고 불러오다

> Would you please **bring** a glass of water to me?
> Don't forget to **take** your umbrella when you leave.
> You had better go and **fetch** a doctor.

22. 주요 기본동사와 함께 쓰는 관용어구

1) do를 쓰는 관용어구

do one's work 일하다
do one's homework 숙제하다
do one's duty 의무를 다하다
do one's best 최선을 다하다
do the dishes 설거지하다
do the laundry 세탁하다
do one's hair 머리를 손질하다
do one's military service 병역을 이행하다
do good[harm/ damage] to ~에 이익[손해]이 되다
do somebody a favor ~에게 호의를 베풀다

2) make를 쓰는 관용어구

make an appointment 약속하다
make an attempt 시도하다
make a call 전화하다
make a decision 결정하다
make a choice 선택하다
make an offer 신청하다
make a contribution 공헌하다
make an effort 노력하다
make a mistake 실수하다
make a speech 연설하다
make a fortune 재산을 모으다
make money 돈을 벌다
make an impression 인상을 주다
make a profit 이익을 얻다
make a noise 떠들다
make progress 진보하다
make a reservation 예약하다
make sense 이치에 맞다, 말이 되다
make up one's mind 결심하다
make a difference 차이가 생기다; 중요하다

3) have를 쓰는 관용어구

have breakfast[dinner] 식사하다
have a hard time 고생하다(= have trouble)
have a try 시험해보다
have a headache[stomachache/ toothache] 두통[복통, 치통]이 있다
have a cold 감기에 걸리다
have an effect[influence] on ~에 영향을 주다

4) take를 쓰는 관용어구

> take a chance 위험을 감수하다, 기회를 잡다
> take pains 수고하다
> take part in ~에 참가하다, 참여하다
> take place 발생하다
> take a rest 휴식하다
> take an examination 시험을 치르다
> take a risk 위험을 무릅쓰다
> take medication 약을 복용하다

5) 기타 관용어구

> bear fruits 결실을 보다[맺다]
> catch a cold 감기에 걸리다
> shed tears 눈물을 흘리다
> keep a diary 일기를 쓰다

시제(Tense)

1. 현재

1) 현재의 사실/동작/상태/습관/반복적인 행위

주로 always, usually, in the morning, as a rule 등의 표현과 함께 쓴다.

He **speaks** English very well.
I **love** her from the bottom of my heart.
She always **comes** to the class late. <현재의 습관>
He **lives** in New York City. <현재, 지속적인 거주>

(cf.) He **is living** in New York City. 〈현재 진행, 일시적인 거주〉

2) 영속적인 불변의 진리/사실/속담/격언

Two and five **is** seven.
The sun **rises** in the east.
The Mississippi **is** one of the longest rivers in the world.
The early bird **catches** the worm. <속담>

3) 미래시제의 대용

① 시간, 조건을 나타내는 부사절에서는 미래시제 대신 현재시제를 사용한다.

I will write to you *when* I **get** to Vancouver.
We will start *as soon as* she **comes** back.
If she **comes** tomorrow, we will take her with us.
He will not do it *unless* you **pay** him.

(cf.) I want to know *if* he **will come** to the party. 〈명사절〉
　　　Tell me the time *when* he **will come** back. 〈형용사절〉

② '왕래발착동사 + 미래표시어구'가 쓰여 가까운 미래의 확실한 예정을 나타낼 때, 현재시제로 미래시제를 대용한다.

Father **comes** home *tomorrow* from the trip.
The World Cup **begins** *next month*.

2. 과거

1) 과거의 사실/상태/동작/경험/습관/역사적인 사실

It **was** cold *yesterday*.
He **left** *an hour ago*.
Columbus **discovered** America *in 1492*.

(cf.) '과거의 습관'을 나타내는 표현
　　　He **would** often **ask** me some odd questions. 〈불규칙적인 습관〉
　　　He **used to take a walk** every early morning. 〈규칙적인 습관〉
　　　There **used to be** a pond over there. 〈과거 한때의 상태〉

2) 과거시제와 함께 쓰이는 부사구

yesterday, just now, the day before yesterday, the other day, when I was young, 'last + 시점', '기간 + ago', 'that[those] + 시점' 등의 명백한 과거 시점을 나타내는 부사구가 있으면 반드시 과거시제를 써야 한다.

I **was** born *in 1979*.
He **died** *ten years ago*.
She **screamed** *when she saw a mouse*.
I **met** her *the day before yesterday*.

(cf.) ago와 before의 차이
- ago는 단독으로 쓸 수 없고, 항상 '시간 + ago'의 형태로 과거시제와 함께 쓴다.
- before는 단독으로 과거, 현재완료, 과거완료에 모두 쓰이며, '시간 + before'의 형태일 때는 과거완료와 함께 쓴다.

I **saw** him for the first time *ten years ago*.
I **haven't met** her *before*.
I **had met** her *two years before*.

3) 현재완료 대용

already, before, ever, just, lately, never, often, recently 등의 완료표시 부사가 있는 경우 과거시제를 써서 현재완료를 나타낼 수 있다. 주로 과거의 경험을 나타낸다.

Did you *ever* see a zebra?
= **Have** you *ever* **seen** a zebra?
I never **saw** her *recently*.
= I **have** never **seen** her *recently*.

4) 과거완료 대용

시간의 전후관계가 명확할 때나 과거의 일을 시간 순서로 나열할 경우에는 과거완료 대신 과거시제를 쓸 수 있다.

All the guests **(had) left** *before* she came.
After he **(had) finished** his homework, he began to read the novel.

3. 미래

1) 단순미래

때가 되면 자연히 그렇게 되어가는 것을 표현하는 것으로, 모든 인칭에 will을 사용한다. 문어체 또는 영국영어에서는 1인칭에 shall을 쓰기도 한다.

I **will[shall]** be 30 years old in January.
Will he call me tomorrow?

2) 의지미래

사람의 의지에 의해 좌우될 수 있는 미래로, 평서문에서는 말하는 사람의 의지, 즉 '나(I)'의 의지를 나타내고, 의문문에서는 말을 듣는 상대방, 즉 '당신(you)'의 의지(의사)를 묻는다.

① 평서문: 화자의 의지를 나타내는 경우
   1인칭에는 will을 쓰고 2인칭, 3인칭에는 shall을 쓴다.

> I **will** finish the work by tomorrow.
> You **shall** have this book.
> = I **will** give you this book.
> He **shall** go there at once.
> = I **will** make him go there at once.

② 의문문: 청자의 의지를 묻는 경우
   1인칭, 3인칭에는 shall을 쓰고 2인칭에는 will을 쓴다.

> **Shall** I open the window?
> **Will** you have some more coffee?
> **Shall** he come here?
> = **Shall** I make him come here?

3) 미래 대용 표현

① be going to + 동사원형 ~할 예정[작정]이다

> It **is going to** rain tomorrow.
> I **am going to** buy a tablet PC soon.

② be about to + 동사원형 막 ~하려고 하고 있다

> We **were about to** leave, when it rained.

③ be to + 동사원형 ~할 예정이다 <be to용법 중 예정>

> He **is to** come here tonight.

④ be + 형용사 + to + 동사원형
   bound, due, likely, supposed 등

The Prime Minister **is due to** speak tomorrow.
My friend **is supposed to** arrive here at nine.

4. 현재완료

1) 현재완료의 용법

과거의 일이 현재에 영향을 미칠 때 현재완료시제를 사용한다.

① 완료: 현재까지의 동작의 완료 (지금 막 ~했다)
just, already, yet 등의 부사와 주로 함께 쓰인다.

He **has** *just* **gone** out.
She **has** *already* **read** the book.
I **have** not **seen** her *yet*.

② 경험: 과거 어느 때부터 현재까지의 경험 (~한 적이 있다)
before, ever, never, often, once, seldom, sometimes, lately, recently 등의 빈도표시 부사와 함께 주로 쓰인다.

Have you *ever* **been** to Rome?
I **have** *never* **visited** a foreign country.
I **have read** the book *once*.
He **has had** a lot of bad luck *lately/ recently*.

③ 결과: 과거에 이루어진 행위의 결과가 현재까지 미치고 있는 상태
(~했다. 그 결과 지금은 …이다)

Someone **has broken** the window.
I **have lost** my smartphone.
= I lost my smartphone and I don't have it now.

(cf.) I **lost** my smartphone. 〈현재 다시 찾았는지 혹은 새로 구입했는지 알 수 없다.〉
(cf.) have been to + 장소 vs. have gone to + 장소
She **has been to** Paris. 〈경험, 그녀는 파리에 가본 적이 있다.〉
She **has gone to** Paris. 〈결과, 그녀는 파리에 가고 없다.〉

④ 계속: 과거에 시작된 행위가 현재까지 이어지는 상태 (현재까지 ~해오고 있다)
'since + 시점/절', 'for + 기간', 'during[in/ for/ over] the last[past] + 기간', 'so far', 'up to now', 'until now' 등의 표현과 함께 쓴다.

We **haven't had** any trouble *so far*.
You**'ve been** so good *up to now*.
I **have lived** here in Seoul *since I was born*.
<since절은 과거시제, since는 접속사>
I **have worked** in KAL *since 2008*. <since + 시점, since는 전치사>
I **have worked** in KAL *since 3 years ago*.
= I **have worked** in KAL *for 3 year*s.

(cf.) I **worked** in KAL *for 3 years*. 〈현재는 근무하고 있지 않음〉

2) 현재완료시제를 쓸 수 없는 경우

① 과거시점을 나타내는 부사, 부사구(절)이 있는 경우

I ***have seen** Mary *a week ago*. (×)
I **saw** Mary *a week ago*. (○)

② 의문사 when과 함께

When ***has** he **come** back? (×)
When **did** he **come** back? (○)

③ just now와 함께

He ***has left** here *just now*. (×)
He **left** here *just now*. (○)

5. 과거완료

1) 과거완료의 용법

특정 과거 시점까지의 동작의 완료, 결과, 경험, 계속을 나타낸다.

① 완료

When I **had finished** my homework, I went out for a walk.

② 결과

Spring **had gone** again by the time she was well.

③ 경험

I **had** never **seen** her before.

④ 계속

I **had lived** here for ten years before I moved to Suwon.

2) 대과거

과거 어느 시점 이전에 발생한 일을 과거완료시제로 나타낸다.

I **found** that I **had lost** my watch.
My mother **sent** me a coat that she **had bought** in Vancouver.
She **could not sleep** well because she **had had** much coffee.

(cf.) 사건이 발생한 순서대로 쓴 경우와 after와 before로 인해 전후관계가 분명한 경우에는 과거완료 대신에 과거시제를 쓸 수 있다.
My boyfriend **bought** me a diamond ring *and* I **lost** it.
The train **left**(= **had left**) *before* we **reached** the station.
My son **went** out *after* he **finished**(= **had finished**) his homework.

3) 과거에 실현되지 못한 기대/희망/의도/욕망의 표현

expect, hope, intend, wish 등의 '과거완료형 + 단순부정사' 또는 '과거형 + 완료부정사' 형태는 과거에 실현되지 못한 일을 나타낸다.

I **had hoped to see** the show.
= I **hoped to have seen** the show.
= I hoped to see the movie, but I couldn't. (그 공연을 보았으면 좋았을 텐데.)

4) by the time S + V(과거), S + had + p.p.

By the time we **got** to the airport, our plane **had** already **left**.
By the time the doctor **arrived,** the patient **had** already **died**.

5) scarcely[hardly] ~ when[before] …
  hardly[scarcely] + 과거완료 + when[before] + 과거
  = no sooner + 과거완료 + than + 과거
  = as soon as + 과거 + 과거

> They **had scarcely seen** a policeman come **when[before]** they **ran** away.
> = They **had no sooner seen** a policeman come **than** they **ran** away.
> = **No sooner had** they **seen** a policeman come **than** they **ran** away.
> = **Scarcely had** they **seen** a policeman come **before** they **ran** away.
> = **As soon as** they saw a policeman come, they **ran** away. <과거 + 과거>
> = **The moment** they saw a policeman come, they **ran** away.
> = **On seeing** a policeman come, they **ran** away.
> (그들은 경찰관이 다가오는 것을 보자마자 도망쳤다.)

6. 미래완료

미래의 어느 때를 기준점으로 그때까지의 완료, 결과, 경험, 계속을 나타낸다.

1) 완료

> She **will have finished** her homework *by ten o'clock.*

2) 결과

> She **will have left** here *by the time you are here.*

3) 경험

> I **will have read** the book four times *if I read it again.*

4) 계속

> *By next June* she **will have lived** in Suwon for six years.

(cf.) 시간, 조건의 부사절에서는 현재완료가 미래완료를 대신한다.
  I will lend you the book *when* I *****will have read** it. (×)
  I will lend you the book *when* I **have read** it. (○)
  If it *****will have rained** for one month, we will float in the ocean. (×)
  If it **has rained** for one month, we will float in the ocean. (○)

7. 진행시제

1) 현재진행시제

현재 시점에서 진행 중인 동작, 상태, 행위의 반복, 가까운 미래의 예정(왕래 발착동사의 경우)을 나타낸다.

> It **is snowing** outside *now*.
> You **are** *always* **finding** fault with me.
> The bus **is coming** soon.

(cf.) 현재시제와 현재진행시제의 차이점
현재시제는 일반적이고 반복적인 행위를 나타내며, 현재진행시제는 한 순간 계속되는 일시적인 행위를 나타낸다.
The girl is nice. (그 소녀는 착하다. 본래 착함)
The girl is being nice. (그 소녀는 착하게 굴고 있다. 현재 시점에서만 착함)

2) 과거진행시제

과거시점에 진행 중이었던 일시적인 동작, 습관, 가까운 미래의 예정을 나타낸다.

> She **was sleeping** when I came home. <일시적인 동작>
> They **were leaving** the next day. <예정>

3) 미래진행시제

미래의 어느 시점에서 진행되고 있을 동작을 나타낸다.

> My father **will be working** on the farm tomorrow.
> He **will be reading** a novel when we go to bed.

4) 진행형으로 쓸 수 없는 동사

```
심리: know, understand, think, believe, intend, want, remember, forget 등
감정: like, love, dislike, hate, fear, mind 등
감각: see, hear, feel[smell/ taste/ sound] + 형용사 등
소유: have, belong to, possess, own, lack 등
형상: resemble, seem[look/ appear] + 형용사 등
존재, 상태 지속: exist, remain[keep/ stay] + 형용사 등
구성, 포함 관계: consist of, contain, include 등
```

He ***is resembling** his mother. (×)
He **resembles** his mother. (○)
These cars ***are belonging to** me. (×)
These cars **belong to** me. (○)

(cf.) '상태'가 아닌 '일시적인 동작'을 나타내는 경우에는 진행형을 쓸 수 있다.
He **is having** dinner.
I'm **thinking of** buying a car.
I **was looking at** the moon.

8. 완료진행시제

1) 현재완료진행

과거 어느 시점에서 시작된 동작이 현재까지 이어지고 있음을 나타낸다.

I **have been reading** the book for five hours.
He **has been waiting** for an hour.

2) 과거완료진행

과거 어느 시점까지의 동작의 계속을 나타낸다.

I **had been reading** the book for five hours when he came.
He **had been sleeping** for two hours when his friend came.

3) 미래완료진행

'(…이면) 계속 ~하고 있는 셈이 된다'라는 의미로, 미래의 어느 시점까지의 동작의 계속을 나타낸다.

I **will have been reading** the book for five hours by noon.
You **will have been studyin**g French for four years by November next year.

9. 시제일치

1) 주절이 현재일 때

종속절은 어느 시제나 가능하다. 단, 과거완료는 원칙적으로 제외한다.

He **says** that he **works** in Samsung.
He **says** that he **has worked** in Samsung.
He **says** that he **worked** in Samsung.
He **says** that he **will work** in Samsung.

2) 주절이 과거일 때

종속절은 과거, 과거완료

He **said** that he *****will see** the movie. (×)
He **said** that he **would see** the movie. <과거에서 본 미래>
He **said** that he **had seen** the movie *three days before*.

3) 시제일치의 예외

① 불변의 진리, 습관, 반복적 행위, 현재까지 미치는 사실은 항상 현재시제

He **said** that the earth **is** round.
Dad always **told** me that honesty **is** the best policy.
He **told** us that he **gets** up at 6 all the year round.
He **told** me yesterday that he **is** 11 years old.

② 역사적 사실은 항상 과거시제

The teacher **said** that the Korean War **broke out** in 1950.
He **said** that Milton **was born** in 1608.
I **learned** in high school Columbus **discovered** the New World first in 1492.

③ 가정법 동사는 주절 동사의 영향을 받지 않는다.

He **said**, "if I **were** a bird, I **could fly** to you."
→ He **said** that if he **were** a bird, he **could fly** to me.

④ 주절 동사가 과거인 경우 'must, ought to, need not, had better + 동사원형'은 종속절에서 그대로 쓴다.

> They **said** that you **must go out and have** fun as much as you could.
> They **said** that you **ought to go out and have** fun as much as you could.
> They **said** that you **need not go out and have** fun as much as you could.
> They **said** that you **had better go** out and have fun as much as you could.

(cf.) must의 경우, 주절에서는 시제에 일치시켜 쓴다.
  Yesterday he ***must*** go there. (×)
  Yesterday he **had to** go there. (○)
  We ***must*** leave *tomorrow morning*. (×)
  We **will have to** leave *tomorrow morning*. (○)

수동태(Passive Voice)

1. 수동태의 시제

완료형: have been p.p.
진행형: be being p.p.
조동사를 포함한 경우: 조동사 + be p.p.

1) 현재

He **makes** a doll.
→ A doll **is made** by him.

2) 과거

He **made** a doll.
→ A doll **was made** by him.

3) 미래

He **will make** a doll.
→ A doll **will be made** by him.

4) 현재완료

He **has made** a doll.
→ A doll **has been made** by him.

5) 과거완료

He **had made** a doll.
→ A doll **had been made** by him.

6) 미래완료

He **will have made** a doll.
→ A doll **will have been made** by him.

7) 현재진행

He **is making** a doll.
→ A doll **is being made** by him.

8) 과거진행

He **was making** a doll.
→ A doll **was being made** by him.

(cf.) 미래진행형, 현재완료진행형, 과거완료진행형, 미래완료진행형의 수동태는 거의 사용하지 않는다.

2. 수동태 불가 동사

1) 자동사

exist, appear(나타나다), disappear, occur, happen, originate(시작되다), turn up(나타나다), live, rise, grow, remain, seem, appear(~인 것 같다) 등

The accident ***was occurred** around 11 o'clock last night. (×)
The accident **occurred** around 11 o'clock last night. (○)
The little boy ***was disappeared** down the road. (×)
The little boy **disappeared** down the road. (○)

2) 타동사 일부

have(소유), possess, belong to(소속), lack(없다, 부족하다), resemble, suit(어울리다), meet(만나다), consist of, graduate from, result in/ from 등

> Her mother *is resembled by the girl. (×)
> The girl resembles her mother. (○)
> The car *is belonged to my father. (×)
> The car belongs to my father. (○)

3. 3형식 동사의 수동태

1) 목적어가 명사, 대명사일 때

> He opened the door.
> → The door was opened by him.
> The soldiers killed him in the battle.
> → He was killed by the soldiers in the battle.

2) 목적어가 that절일 때

believe, consider, expect, say, suppose, think 등
일반주어 + believe + that + S + V
→ It is believed that + S + V
→ S + is believed to V

> People thought[believed/ supposed/ said] that she was the best singer.
> = It was thought[believed/ supposed/ said] that she was the best singer.
> = She was thought[believed/ supposed/ said] to be the best singer.

(cf.) that절의 주어를 수동태의 주어로 할 경우, 주절의 시제와 that 이하 종속절의 시제가 같으면 단순 부정사를 쓰고, that 이하 종속절의 시제가 주절의 시제보다 한 시제 앞서면 완료 부정사의 형태로 쓴다.
  It is believed that she knew the truth about tobacco.
  → She is believed to have known the truth about tobacco.
  She said that the broker had been a liar.
  → The broker was said to have been a liar.

(cf.) 'tell + 목적어 + that절'의 수동태
  They told me that she was very beautiful.
  → I was told that she was very beautiful.

4. 4형식 동사의 수동태

1) 간접목적어, 직접목적어 모두를 수동태의 주어로 하는 동사

ask, give, show, teach, tell 등

She **gave** *me the book*.
→ *I* **was given** the book by her.
   The book **was given** (to) me by her.
She **taught** *them English*.
→ *They* **were taught** English by her.
   English **was taught** (to) them by her.
He **asked** me a *question*.
→ *I* **was asked** a question by him.
   A question **was asked** of me by him.

2) 직접목적어만을 수동태의 주어로 하는 동사

bring, buy, get, hand, make, read, sell, send, write 등

She **wrote** me *a letter*.
→ *A letter* **was written** (to) me by her. (○)
   *I was written a letter by her. (×)
They **bought** me *some neckties*.
→ *Some neckties* **were bought** for me by them. (○)
   *I was bought some neckties by them. (×)

3) 간접목적어만을 수동태의 주어로 하는 동사

envy, save, spare 등

They **envied** *him* his good looks.
→ *He* **was envied** his good looks by them. (○)
*His good looks were envied him by them. (×)

5. 5형식 동사의 수동태

1) V + O + 명사/형용사

They **elected** him *president*.
→ He **was elected** *president* by them.
Many candidates **found** this question *difficult*.
→ This question **was found** *difficult* by many candidates.

2) V + O + to부정사

The company **forced** her *to resign*.
→ She **was forced** *to resign* by the company.
He **asked** me *to visit* him sometime.
→ I **was asked** *to visit* him sometime by him.

3) V + O + as + 명사/형용사

We **regard** Einstein **as** *one of the foremost scientists*.
→ Einstein **is regarded as** *one of the foremost scientists*.

4) 지각/사역동사

목적격 보어로 쓰인 원형부정사가 수동태 문장에서는 to부정사가 된다.

He **made** her *sing* a song. <사역동사>
→ She **was made** *to sing* a song by him.
We **saw** her *enter* the store with her husband. <지각동사>
→ She **was seen** *to enter* the store with her husband (by us).

5) let + O + 동사원형

He **let** her sing a song.
→ She **was allowed to sing** a song by him.
→ He **let a song be sung** by her.

6) have + O + 동사원형

> She **had** him carry her suitcase.
> → She **had her suitcase carried** by him. (○)
> *He was had to carry her suitcase by her. (×)

6. 상태수동과 동작수동

1) 상태수동

be[lie/ remain/ rest/ stand] + p.p. <주어의 상태 강조>

> She **is married** to a pilot.
> He **lay buried** under the snow.
> Our house **is painted** green.

2) 동작수동

become[get/ grow] + p.p. <주어의 동작 강조: ~하게 되다>

> His secret **became known** to everybody.
> You will soon **grow accustomed** to it.

7. 능동형 수동태

능동형으로 쓰이지만 수동의 의미로 해석한다.

1) 자동사

peel, print, read, say, sell, wash, write 등
주로 부사와 함께 능동형으로 쓰여 수동의 의미를 나타낸다.

> Your report **reads** well. <읽히다>
> The new car **is selling** badly. <팔리다>

2) 능동의 부정사

to blame, to let 등

> He is **to blame** for the accident.
> = He is **to be blamed** for the accident.
> This room is **to let**.
> = This room is **to be let**. (세를 놓을 방이다)

3) 능동의 동명사

사물 주어 다음에 쓰인 'be worth/ deserve/ need/ require/ want + 능동의 동명사'는 수동의 의미를 나타낸다.

> The movie **is worth watching** all over again. (= is worth to be watched)
> The problem **deserves solving**. (= deserves to be solved)
> The fence **needs fixing**. (= needs to be fixed)

8. 부정주어 구문의 수동태

부정주어(Nobody/ Nothing)는 수동태 문장에서 'not ~ by anybody', 'not ~ by anything'이 된다.

> *Nobody* helped him.
> → He **was** *not* **helped** *by anybody*. (○)
> → He **was helped** **by nobody*. (×)

9. 동사구의 수동태

동사구 전체를 하나의 타동사로 취급하여 수동태로 전환한다.

1) 자동사 + 전치사

account for, ask for, attend to, deal with, depend on, laugh at, look after, rely on, run over, speak to 등

> The audience **laughed at** him.
> → He **was laughed at by** the audience.
> A car **ran over** his dog.
> → His dog **was run over by** a car.

2) 자동사 + 부사 + 전치사

catch up with, do away with, look down upon, look forward to, look up to, put up with, speak ill[well] of 등

The villagers **looked down upon** him.
→ He **was looked down upon by** the villagers.
They **speak well of** him.
→ He **is well spoken of** (by them).
The Russian **was caught up with by** the police.
The death penalty **has been done away with** (by them) in many countries.

3) 타동사 + 명사 + 전치사

catch sight of, get rid of, make use of, pay attention to, take care of, take notice of 등

The government **took notice of** their opinions.
→ Their opinions **was taken notice of by** the government.
He **took good care of** the orphan. <명사 앞에 수식어가 있는 경우>
→ The orphan **was taken good care of** by him.
→ **Good care was taken of** the orphan by him.

10. 의문문의 수동태

1) 의문사가 있는 경우

① 의문사가 주어인 경우: By 의문사(목적격) + be + S + p.p.

Who built the Great Wall?
→ **By whom was** the Great Wall **built**?
Who showed you the way to the university?
→ **By whom were** you **shown** the way to the university?

② 의문사가 주어가 아닌 경우: 의문사 + be + p.p. + (by 행위자)

What did she discover?
→ **What was discovered** by her?
When did you finish the report?
→ **When was** the report **finished** by you?

2) 의문사가 없는 경우: be + 주어 + p.p. + (by 행위자)

> Does she love him?
> → **Is** he **loved** by her?
> Did he break the windows?
> → **Were** the windows **broken** by him?

11. 명령문의 수동태

긍정문: Let + 목적어 + be + p.p.
부정문: Don't let + 목적어 + be + p.p./ Let + 목적어 + not + be + p.p.

> Write your name on this paper.
> → **Let** your name **be written** on this paper.
> Don't forget this advice.
> → **Don't let** this advice **be forgotten**.
> → **Let** this advice **not be forgotten**.

12. 수동태 형태의 관용표현

1) be amazed at, be astonished at, be surprised at ~에 놀라다

> He **was surprised at** her conduct.

2) be amused with, be delighted with, be pleased with
~에 기뻐하다, 즐거워하다

> They **were pleased with** your success.

3) be contented with, be satisfied with ~에 만족하다

> She **is satisfied with** the current job.

4) be disappointed at[with] ~에 실망하다

> They **were disappointed at** the result of the game.
> He **was disappointed with** last month's profits.

5) be bored with, be fed up with ~에 싫증나다, 질리다

> He **was fed up with** her complaining.

6) be assured of, be convinced of ~을 확신하다

> The lawyer **is convinced of** the innocence of the prisoner.

7) be offended at, be annoyed at ~에 화내다

> He **was annoyed at** her stupidity.

8) be concerned about ~을 걱정하다
   be concerned with ~와 관련되다

> We **are concerned about** preserving our natural resources.
> This is not the type of a problem I should **be concerned with**.

9) be ashamed of ~을 부끄러워하다

> He **was ashamed of** his laziness.

10) be addicted to ~에 빠져 있다, 중독되다

> Ashley **is addicted to** cocaine and heroine.

11) be engaged in ~에 종사하다
    be engaged to ~와 약혼 중이다

> We **are engaged in** a variety of English education fields.
> His daughter **was engaged to** a lawyer.

12) be devoted to, be committed to, be dedicated to ~에 전념하다, ~에 헌신하다

She **was devoted to** bringing up children.
He **was dedicated to** his patients.

13) be absorbed in, be engrossed in, be immersed in ~에 몰두하다, 열중하다

A child **is absorbed in** playing with his blocks.

14) be involved in ~에 관련되다

They **are involved in** drug dealing.

15) be interested in ~에 관심이 있다

She **was interested in** working with computers.

16) be accustomed to, be used to ~에 익숙하다

She **is accustomed to** frugal lifestyle.

17) be married to ~와 결혼하다

The actress **was married to** a film producer.

18) be covered with ~으로 덮여 있다

The entire mountain **is covered with** cherry blossoms.

19) be acquainted with ~에 정통하다, 잘 알다

The students **are acquainted with** the works of Shakespeare.

20) be based (up)on, be founded (up)on ~에 기초하다, ~을 토대로 하다

This novel **is based on** personal experience.

21) be located in[at/ on], be situated in[at/ on] ~에 위치하다

The University **is located in** the capital of the country.

22) be tired from ~로 피곤하다
be tired of ~에 싫증나다, 질리다

I **was tired from** a long walk.
I **am tired of** eating the same thing every day.

23) be caught in (비 따위)를 만나다

He **was caught in** a shower on the way.

24) be occupied with ~에 종사[전념]하다

She **was occupied with** studying.

25) be composed of ~으로 구성되다

Water **is composed of** hydrogen and oxygen.

26) be confronted with[by], be faced with[by] ~에 직면하다

Every day we **are confronted with** problems.

27) be associated with ~와 관련되다

Certain stress hormones may **be associated with** alcoholism.

28) be dressed in (옷을) 입다

He **was dressed in** a black suit.

29) be drowned in 익사하다

He **was drowned in** the pond.

30) be embarrassed by, be confused by ~에 당황하다

He **was embarrassed by** lack of money.

31) be exposed to ~에 노출되다

Many people **were exposed to** danger.

32) be filled with ~로 가득 차 있다

The classroom **is filled with** students.

33) be impressed with ~에 감명을 받다

I **was** deeply **impressed with** his speech.

34) be indulged in ~에 빠지다, 탐닉하다

He **was indulged in** gambling.

35) be opposed to ~에 반대하다

He **was opposed to** her idea.

36) be possessed of ~을 소유하다
    be possessed with[by] ~에 사로잡히다

She **is possessed of** great wealth.
He **is possessed with** an evil spirit.

37) be related to ~와 관계가 있다

A language **is** closely **related to** the culture.

38) be sentenced to ~의 선고를 받다

> He **was sentenced to** death at the trial.

39) be subjected to ~을 받다, 당하다, 시달리다

> Black people **are** still **subjected to** social discrimination.

40) be condemned to ~하도록 운명 지워지다

> Jesus **was condemned to** death.

41) be made of (물리적 변화) ~으로 만들어지다
    be made from (화학적 변화) ~으로 만들어지다

> This chair **is made of** wood.
> Tea, cocoa and coffee **are made from** plants that contain caffeine.

42) be known + 전치사 잘 알려져 있다
    be known to + 대상
    be known as + 자격
    be known for + 이유
    be known by + 판단의 근거

> The musician **is known to** everybody.
> He **is known as** an active man who enjoys hiking and cycling.
> Hokkaido **is known for** deep snow in winter.
> A man **is known by** the company he keeps.

가정법
(Subjunctive Mood)

1. 가정법 현재

현재나 미래의 불확실한 일을 가정, 상상하는 경우에 쓴다.
If + S + V(현재동사/동사원형), S + will[shall/ can/ may] + V

> If he **is** honest, I **will employ** him.
> If I **have** enough money next year, I **will go** to Rome.
> If it **is/ be** fine tomorrow, we **can go** fishing.

2. 가정법 미래

1) 미래에 실현될 가능성이 거의 희박한 일에 대한 가정과 상상을 나타내는 경우

   If + S + should + V, S + would[should/ could/ might] + V
                                will[shall/ can/ may]

   > If it **should not rain** tomorrow, I **would go** out.
   > If she **should call**, I**'ll ring back.**

2) 미래의 실현 불가능한 일을 가정하는 경우

If + S + were to + V, S + would[should/ could/ might] + V

If I **were to be born** again, I **would be** a singer.
If the sun **were to rise** in the west, I **would not change** my mind.

(cf.) 주어의 의지를 나타낼 때에는 if절에 would를 쓴다.
If you **would** help me, I would be grateful.
If you **would** succeed, you would have to work hard.

3. 가정법 과거

현재 사실과 반대되는 상황을 가정하거나 상상할 때 쓴다.
If + S + V(과거동사), S + would[should/ could/ might] + V
(조건절의 동사로 be동사가 올 경우에는 were를 쓴다.)

If I **were** healthy, I **could go** there.
= As I am not healthy, I cannot go there.
If it **didn't rain** now, we **could play** baseball.
If I **had** enough money now, I **would go** to Rome.
If I **were** a bird, I **would fly** to you.

4. 가정법 과거완료

과거의 사실과 반대되는 상황을 가정하거나 상상할 때 쓴다.
If + S + had p.p., S + would[should/ could/ might] + have p.p.

If he **had been** honest, I **would have employed** him.
= As he was not honest, I didn't employ him.
If you **had studied** harder last year, you **would have passed** the exam.
If I **had known** the answer, I **could have helped** you.
If it **had not snowed** yesterday, we **would have gone out**.

5. 혼합가정법

과거의 사실이나 사건의 결과가 현재에 영향을 미치는 상황을 가정한다. 주로 주절에 현재 시간을 나타내는 now, today, this morning 등의 부사어구가 쓰인다.
If + S + had p.p., S + would[should/ could/ might] + V

> If it **had not rained** *last night*, the road **would not be** muddy *now*.
> If I **had taken** the plane *then*, I **wouldn't be** alive *now*.

(cf.) If I **had taken** the plane *then*, I **would have been killed** in the air crash.
〈가정법 과거완료〉

6. if 생략 구문

가정법의 if절 안에 were, had, should가 있는 경우 if를 생략할 수 있다. 이때 주어와 동사가 도치된다.

> If you had followed my advice, you would not have failed.
> = **Had you followed** my advice, you would not have failed.
> **If I were** you, I would not do such a thing.
> = **Were I** you, I would not do such a thing.
> **If anyone should call**, please take a message.
> = **Should anyone call**, please take a message.

7. I wish + 가정법

1) I wish + 가정법 과거

I wish 다음에 가정법 과거 문장이 오면 현재 사실에 반대되는 소망을 나타낸다. 종속절의 시제는 주절의 시제와 같으며, 종속절에 be동사가 올 경우에는 were를 써야 한다.

> **I wish** I **were** rich.
> = I am sorry (that) I am not rich.
> **I wished** I **were** rich.
> = I was sorry (that) I was not rich.

2) I wish + 가정법 과거완료

과거 사실에 반대되는 소망을 나타낸다. 종속절의 시제는 주절의 시제보다 한 시제 앞선다.

> **I wish** I **had been** rich.
> = I am sorry (that) I was not rich.
> **I wished** I **had been** rich.
> = I was sorry (that) I had not been rich.

(cf.) I wish + S + would 〈미래의 소망〉
    I **wish** she **would come** to my house.

(cf.) I wish 뒤에 조동사의 과거형, 조동사의 과거형 + have p.p.도 올 수 있다.
    I **wish** I **could go** to the concert with you tomorrow.
    I **wish** you **could have come** to the party yesterday.

3) I wish의 대용 어구

> **I wish** I **were** a bird.
> = **If only** I **were** a bird.
> = **Would (that)** I **were** a bird.

8. It's (about/ high) time + 가정법 과거

(늦었지만) 이제는 ~해야 할 시간이다

> **It is about time** you **went** to bed.
> = It is time you should go to bed.
> = It is time (for you) to go to bed.
> **It is high time** you **started** looking for a job.
> = It is time you should start looking for a job.
> = It is time (for you) to start looking for a job.

9. as if[though] + 가정법

1) as if[though] + 가정법 과거 마치 ~인 것처럼 <주절의 시제와 같은 시제>

> He *speaks* English well **as if** he **were** an American.
> The boy *talks* **as if** he **knew** everything.
> The boy *talked* **as if** he **knew** everything.

2) as if[though] + 가정법 과거완료 마치 ~였던 것처럼 <주절의 시제보다 앞선 시제>

> He *acts* **as if** he **had been** the boss.
> He *looks* **as if** he **had seen** a ghost.
> He *looked* **as if** he **had seen** a ghost.

(cf.) It looks **as if** it's going to snow. 〈as if 뒤에 직설법 현재가 오기도 함〉

10. but for/ without

1) but for[without] + N, + 가정법 과거 주절
~이 없다면(= if it were not for ~, were it not for ~)

> **But for** water, we **could not live**.
> = **Without** water, we **could not live**.
> = **If it were not for** water, we **could not live**.
> = **Were it not for** water, we **could not live**. <if 생략에 따른 도치>

2) but for[without] + N, + 가정법 과거완료 주절
~이 없었더라면(= if it had not been for ~, had it not been for ~)

> **But for** your advice, I **would have failed**.
> = **Without** your advice, I **would have failed**.
> = **If it had not been for** your advice, I **would have failed**.
> = **Had it not been for** your advice, I **would have failed**.
> <if 생략에 따른 도치>

11. would rather/ would sooner + 가정법

1) S + would rather[would sooner] + (that) + S + 가정법 과거
차라리[오히려] ~라면 좋겠는데

> I **would rather** you **came** tomorrow.
> I**'d sooner** you **paid** me now.

2) S + would rather[would sooner] + (that) + S + 가정법 과거완료
차라리[오히려] ~이었더라면 좋겠는데

> I **would rather** I **had gone** to school yesterday.
> I **would sooner** he **hadn't told** me about it.

12. 직설법 + otherwise + 가정법

otherwise는 if ~ not/ or else의 뜻으로 쓰이며, 부정의 조건절 전체를 대신한다.

1) 직설법 현재 + otherwise + 가정법 과거

> I **am** busy; **otherwise** I **would help** you.
> = I am busy; if I were not busy, I would help you.

2) 직설법 과거 + otherwise + 가정법 과거완료

> I **used** my calculator; **otherwise** I**'d have taken** longer.
> = I used my calculator; if I hadn't used my calculator, I'd have taken longer.

13. 가정법 + but/ except/ save (that) + 직설법

1) 가정법 과거 + but[except/ save] (that) + 직설법 현재
~하지만 않으면

> I **would help** you **but that** I **am** busy. <현재 실제로 바쁨>
> = I would help you if I were not busy.

2) 가정법 과거완료 + but[except/ save] (that) + 직설법 과거
~하지 않았었다면

> I **would have called** you up **but that** I **didn't know** your number.
> <실제로 번호를 몰랐음>
> = I would have called you up if I had known your number.

14. What if + 가정법/직설법

~라면[하면] 어쩌지?(= What would[will] happen if ~)

> **What if** I **should fail** in the entrance exam?
> **What if** it **rains** tomorrow?

15. if절이 없는 가정법 현재

1) S + 주장/제안/요구/명령/충고의 동사 + that + S + (should) + 동사원형
   insist, assert, maintain, propose, move, suggest, demand, require, order, ask 등

> He **insists** that Jason **(should) go** there at once.
> I strongly **suggested** that he **(should) prepare** for his interview.
> The committee **asked** that this project **(should) be** stopped for now.

(cf.) 위의 동사가 당위의 표현이 아닌 경우에는 that절의 동사는 직설법 시제를 따른다.
> He **insisted** that my new composition **was** a plagiarism. 〈사실에 대한 주장〉
> Her letter **suggests** that she **loves** him. 〈'암시하다'라는 의미〉

2) It is + 이성적 판단을 나타내는 형용사 + that + S + (should) + 동사원형
   advisable, essential, imperative, important, natural, necessary, urgent, vital 등

> It is **necessary** that you **(should) do** the task.
> It is **imperative** that colleges **(should) improve** quality of education.

3) 명령·요망의 명사 + that + S + (should) + 동사원형
   명사와 동격을 이루는 that절

   He made the **suggestion** that they **(should) go** there.

16. 문장의 일부에 가정의 의미가 내재되어 있는 경우

A true friend **would not say** such a thing. <주어>
= If he were a true friend, he would not say such a thing.
The professor **would not do** such a thing *in my place*. <부사구>
= The professor would not do such a thing if he were in my place.

조동사
(Auxiliary Verb)

1. can

1) 가능, 능력(= be able to)

He **can** write with either hand
She **can** count up to 10 in Italian.

(cf.) can은 사람, 사물 주어가 모두 가능하지만 be able to는 사람 주어를 원칙으로 하며, 미래와 완료형일 경우 can 대신 be able to가 쓰인다.
He is so strong that he **will be able to** endure any difficulties.
We **have been able to** reach an agreement.

2) 추측, 강한 의혹: 의문문이나 부정문에서

Can it be true?
His story **cannot be** false. <현재의 추측>
= It is impossible that his story is false.
She **cannot have written** the letter. <과거의 추측>
= It is impossible that she wrote the letter.

3) 허가

Can I give you a ring tonight?
Could I borrow your calculator for a moment? <정중한 표현>

2. must

1) 필요, 의무

> You **must** come.
> = You **have to** come.
> Man **must** have food, clothing, and shelter to live.
> One **must** be able to adjust to the changes.

(cf.) must는 과거, 미래시제에 쓰이지 않는다. have to를 사용하여 과거는 had to, 미래는 will have to로 나타낸다. 단, 종속절에서는 must를 과거시제에 사용할 수 있다.
I **had to** walk to the work *yesterday* because my car broke down. 〈과거〉
He **will have to** meet her *tomorrow*. 〈미래〉
He *said* that I **must** stop smoking. 〈종속절〉

2) 강한 추측 (~임에 틀림없다)

> It **must** be raining outside.
> It **must have rained** during the night, for the road is wet. <과거의 강한 추측>

3) must의 부정

불필요: need not, don't have to (~할 필요가 없다)
금지: must not, be not allowed to (~해서는 안 된다)
추측: cannot be (~일 리가 없다)

> You **need not** answer all these questions. <불필요>
> You **must not** drink coffee on an empty stomach. <금지>
> The rumor **cannot be** true; I cannot believe it. <추측>

3. need/ dare

1) 부정문, 의문문에서 조동사로 쓰인다.

> She **need not** *tell* the truth.
> = She doesn't need to tell the truth.
> **Need** he *work* so hard?
> = Does he need to work so hard?
> He **dared not** *look* me in the face.
> = He didn't dare to look me in the face.
> How **dare you** *say* such a thing?
> = How do you dare to say such a thing?

2) 긍정문에서는 본동사로 쓰이며 to부정사를 목적어로 취한다.

> You **need** *to do* this at once.
> She **dared** *to venture* an opinion of her own.

3) need가 긍정문에서 조동사로 쓰이는 경우

need only + 동사원형
All + S + need + 동사원형

> If she wants anything, she **need only** a*sk*.
> **All you need** *do is* (to) listen carefully.

4. used to

1) 과거의 규칙적인 습관 (~하곤 했다)

> He **used to** go fishing with his father.
> When I was younger, my grandmother **used to** make me delicious snacks.

2) 과거의 사실, 상태 (이전에는 ~이 있었다, 전에는 ~이었다)

> There **used to** be a church there.
> He **used to** be a pilot but now he is a hotel manager.

5. will/ would

1) will의 용법

① 주어의 의지

I **will** go with him wherever he goes.
No matter what happens, I **will** do as I please.

② 경향, 습성

Accidents **will** happen.
Dogs **will** bark when they see a stranger.

③ 현재의 불규칙적 습관

He **will** often come to see me these days.
She **will** sit for hours without saying a word.

④ 현재의 고집·거절

She **will** have her own way in everything.
This wood **will** not burn.

2) would의 용법

① 과거의 불규칙적 습관

When I was a boy, I **would** go to school by bicycle.
We **would** often have coffee together.

② 과거의 고집·거절

He **would** not put his coat on.
The horse **would** not move at all.

③ 공손한 표현

> **Would** you get in touch with me in a week?
> **Would** you please show me your boarding pass?

6. should

1) 의무, 당연

> The young **should** respect the old.
> You **should** not speak ill of others.

2) 관용적 용법

> It is *natural* that she (**should**) want to have children. <이성적 판단의 형용사>
> It is *strange* that she (**should**) marry him. <감정적 판단의 형용사>
> She *proposed* that the book (**should**) be banned. <주장·제안의 동사>

7. had better/ would rather

1) had better + 동사원형 ~하는 것이 좋겠다 (= may[might] as well + 동사원형)

> You **had better** *take* your umbrella with you today.
> You **had better** *wait* until the rain stops.

2) would rather + 동사원형 오히려[차라리] ~하겠다
would rather + 동사원형(A) + than + 동사원형(B) B 하느니 차라리 A 하겠다

> I **would rather** *stay* home tonight.
> I **would rather** *die* **than** *live* in dishonor.

3) had better/ would rather의 부정

> You **had better not** go out after dark in New York.
> I **would rather not** mention details.

8. ought to

1) 의무, 당연 (= should)

must보다 약하고 should와 거의 비슷하다.

We **ought to** look up to our parents.
You **ought to** visit him in the hospital.

2) 추측

It **ought to** be rainy tomorrow.
She **ought to** have arrived at his office by now.

3) ought to의 부정

We **ought not to** eat such high fat food.
You **ought not to** go there alone.

9. 조동사 + have p.p

1) 과거의 추측

may[might] have p.p. ~했을지도 모른다
cannot have p.p. ~했을 리가 없다
must have p.p. ~했음에 틀림없다

He **may have met** her.
He **cannot have confessed** his crime.
She **must have forgotten** about the appointment.

2) 과거의 유감

should[ought to] have p.p. ~했어야 했는데
need not have p.p. ~할 필요는 없었는데
would rather have p.p. ~하는 게 좋았을 텐데

You **should have told** me that matter yesterday.
He **need not have attended** the meeting.
She **would rather have stayed** in bed all day.

(cf.) could have p.p. ~할 수도 있었는데 〈가정법 표현〉
would have p.p. ~했을 텐데, 했었을 거야 〈가정법 표현〉
The police **could have found** his fingerprints.
You **would have done** the same for me.

10. 조동사 관용표현

1) may well ~하는 것도 당연하다

You **may well** get angry at his rude words.

2) may[might] as well ~하는 것이 더 낫다
may[might] as well A as B B하는 것보다는 A하는 것이 더 낫다

You **may as well** take a rest.
You **might as well** stay at home **as** go out with him.

3) cannot ~ too 아무리 ~해도 지나치지 않다

People **cannot** be **too** careful in driving a car.

4) have only to ~하기만 하면 된다

You **have only to** do as you were told.

부정사(Infinitive)

1. 명사적 용법

1) 주어

> **To answer** this question is very difficult.
> = **It** is very difficult **to answer** this question. <가주어-진주어 구문>

2) 목적어

① 타동사의 목적어

> I want **to read** this book.

(cf.) I found **it** easy **to read** this book. 〈가목적어-진목적어 구문〉

② 전치사의 목적어
일반적으로 전치사의 목적어는 동명사이지만 but, except, save는 to부정사가 목적어로 쓰인다. 'be about to부정사', 'know better than to부정사', 'have no choice but to부정사' 등의 관용적인 표현에도 유의해야 한다.

> There was nothing for it **but to wait** for a chance.
> I **was about to say** something to him.
> We **have no choice but to hire** additional workers.

③ 의문사 + to부정사

choose, know, learn, show, teach, tell 등의 목적어로는 '의문사 + S + should + V' 구문을 단축한 형태인 '의문사 + to부정사'가 쓰인다.

> He didn't *know* ***to handle** the machine. (×)
> He didn't *know* **how to handle** the machine. (○)
> I don't *know* **what to do**. (= I don't know what I should do.)
> I *taught* him **how to read** English.
> Please *show* me **where to put** my shoes.

3) 보어

① 주격 보어

> To see is **to believe**.
> To do two things at a time is **to do** neither.

② 목적격 보어

> The captain *ordered* his crews **to lower** a sail.
> I *expect* him **to come**.
> You should *get* your friends **to help** you.

2. 형용사적 용법

1) 명사 수식

① 명사가 의미상의 주어

> I have no *friend* **to help** me.
> = I have no friend who helps me.
> He is not *a man* **to forget** such a promise.

② 명사가 의미상의 목적어

> I have no *friend* **to help**.
> = I have no friend (whom) I help.
> Please give me *something* **to drink**.

(cf.) '명사 + to부정사 + 전치사' 구문
앞 명사가 to부정사의 의미상 목적어일 때, 부정사에 쓰인 동사가 자동사이거나 혹은 '타동사 + 목적어'의 형태이면 문미에 전치사가 필요하다.
He has no *house* **to live in**. 〈자동사 live〉
= He has no *house* **in which to live**.
= He has no house which he can live in.
I want *a pen* **to write** a letter **with**. 〈타동사 write + 목적어 a letter〉
= I want *a pen* **with which to write** a letter.

2) 보어

seem, appear, happen, chance + to부정사
come, get, grow + to부정사 ~하게 되다
prove, turn out + to부정사 ~으로 판명 나다

He *seems* **to be** pretty busy.
= It seems that he is pretty busy.
We *happened* **to be** on the same bus.
= It happened that we were on the same bus.
I *got* **to believe** that she was right.
The rumor *turned out* **to be** false.

3) 관용표현

① **the first[the last/ the only/ 최상급] + 명사 + to부정사**
~했던 최초의[결코 ~할 것 같지 않은, 최후의, ~한 유일한, 가장 ~한]

Amundsen was *the first man* **to reach** the South Pole by foot.
He is *the last man* **to tell** a lie.
She is *the only person* **to have won** the award twice.

② **have the + 추상명사 + to부정사**
~하게도 …하다

He *had the kindness* **to help** me.
= He was kind enough to help me.
= He was so kind as to help me.

3. 'be to부정사' 용법

부정사가 명사를 수식하지 않고, 문장 속에서 보어의 역할을 하는 경우를 말한다. 해석은 '의무, 예정, 가능, 의도(의향), 운명'으로 한다.

1) 예정 (~할 것이다)

We **are to meet** at the post office.
They **are to arrive** there at midnight.

2) 의무 (~해야 한다)

You **are to finish** the work by tomorrow.
You **are to clean** the window after dusting.

3) 가능 (~할 수 있다, 주로 수동태로 쓰임)

No one **was to be seen** on the street.
Nothing **is to be had** without perseverance and efforts.

4) 의도 (~하고자 하면, 조건절에서 쓰임)

If you **are to succeed**, you must work hard.
If you **are to remain** here, you should behave much better.

5) 운명 (~할 운명이다, ~하게 되어 있다)

He **was never to see** his wife again.
Byron left his native land, and he **was never to return**.

4. 동격의 부정사

소망, 계획, 결심, 노력, 능력 등의 추상명사는 뒤에 오는 to부정사와 동격 관계이다.
ability, attempt, decision, effort, plan, program, proposal, resolution, wish 등

His *decision* **to retire** surprised all of us.
They devised *a plan* **to reduce** costs.
He made *a resolution* **to quit** smoking.

(cf.) 'of 동명사'를 동격어구로 하는 명사
  hope, idea, possibility, thought, danger, risk, responsibility 등
  He was excited about *the possibility* **of winning** the prize.
  In our cities, young people are growing up without any *hope* **of finding** a job.

(cf.) 'to부정사', 'of 동명사'를 모두 동격어구로 가지는 명사
  chance, way, means, capability, opportunity 등
  I have *a chance* **to go** abroad.
  = I have *a chance* **of going** abroad.

5. 부사적 용법

1) 목적 (~하기 위하여)

> We came here **to study** English.
> We eat **to live**, not live **to eat**.
> He stopped for a minute **to smoke**.

2) 결과 (~해서 …하다)

무의지 동사 awake, live, grow up 뒤에 오거나 'only to부정사', 'never to부정사'의 형태인 경우

> He *awoke* one morning **to find** himself famous.
> Her son *grew up* **to be** the greatest politician.
> He worked hard **only to fail** in the exam.
> = He worked hard but he failed in the exam

3) 감정의 원인 (~해서, ~하니)

감정을 나타내는 동사나 형용사 뒤에 오는 경우

> I'm *sorry* **to trouble** you.
> I was *disappointed* **to find** that they had already left.
> He was *surprised* **to find** the staircase filled with smoke.
> = To his surprise, he found the staircase filled with smoke.

4) 이유, 판단의 근거 (~을 보니, ~하다니)

must be, cannot be, 감탄문 뒤에 오는 경우

> He *must be* honest **to say** so.
> He *cannot be* rich **to ask** you for some money.
> *What a lucky fellow you are* **to have** such a nice girl friend!

5) 조건 (만약 ~한다면)

독립부정사일 경우

I should be very happy **to go** with you.
= I should be very happy **if I could go** with you.

6) 양보 (~하더라도)

To do his best, he could not finish it.
= **Though he did his best**, he could not finish it.

7) 형용사 수식 (~하기에)

English is *difficult* **to learn**.
= It is difficult **to learn** English.
This water is not *good* **to drink**.
= It is not good **to drink** this water.

8) 부사 수식

He is strong *enough* **to protect** himself.
His artwork is not good *enough* **to sell**.

6. 부정사의 의미상의 주어

1) 의미상의 주어를 명시하는 경우

① for + 목적격: 이성적 판단의 형용사 뒤에 올 경우
difficult, hard, impossible, natural, necessary, possible 등

It is *difficult* **for him to solve** the problem.
It is *necessary* **for you to attend** the meeting.
It is *possible* **for me to lend** you a little money.

② of + 목적격: 사람의 성질을 나타내는 형용사 뒤에 올 경우
careful, careless, considerate, cruel, foolish, generous, kind, rude, wise 등

It is very *foolish* **of you to behave** like that.
= You are very foolish to behave like that.
It was very *considerate* **of him to wait**.

2) 의미상의 주어를 명시하지 않는 경우

① 일반인 주어인 경우

It is important **to exercise** regularly.
It is easy **to succumb** to despair.

② 문장의 주어와 일치하거나, 문장의 목적어와 일치하는 경우

I expect **to receive** their report in the near future. <문장의 주어와 일치>
= I expect that I shall receive their report in the near future.
I expect *him* **to become** a successful writer. <문장의 목적어와 일치>
= I expect that he will become a successful writer.

(cf.) 생략된 to부정사의 의미상 주어는 주절의 주어와 일치해야 한다.
To get the job, *skillful English is needed. (×)
To get the job, you[one] must be skillful at English. (○)

7. 부정사의 시제

1) 단순부정사: to + 동사원형

① 본동사와 같은 시제를 나타낸다.

She *seems* **to love** me.
= It seems that she *loves* me.
She *seemed* **to love** me.
= It *seemed* that she *loved* me.

② 미래적 의미

I *hope* **to go** to France.
= I *hope* that I *will go* to France.
She *hoped* **to improve** her grades.
= She *hoped* that she *would improve* her grades.

2) 완료부정사: to + have p.p.

① 본동사보다 한 시제 앞선 시제를 나타낸다.

He *seems* **to have been** ill.
= It *seems* that he *was(has been)* ill.
He *seemed* **to have been** ill.
= It *seemed* that he *had been* ill.

② 과거에 이루지 못한 소망, 기대
   소망, 기대 동사의 과거형 + to have p.p.
   = 소망, 기대 동사의 과거완료형 + 단순부정사

I *hoped* **to have married** her.
= I *had hoped* **to marry** her.
I *intended* **to have called** on her.
= I *had intended* **to call** on her.

8. 부정사의 태

1) 주어를 서술하는 to부정사의 태

We don't want **to help** them. <능동, We가 help하는 행위의 주체>
We don't want **to be helped** by them. <수동, We가 help하는 행위의 대상>

2) 목적어를 서술하는 to부정사의 태

I want you **to type** this letter. <능동, you가 type하는 행위의 주체>
= I want this letter **to be typed**. <수동, this letter가 type하는 행위의 대상>

3) 목적어를 수식하는 to부정사의 태

'have + 목적어 + to부정사'의 형태가 대표적인데, 문장의 주어가 행위의 주체이면 목적어 뒤의 to부정사는 능동태가 원칙이다.

I have a lot of work **to do**. (○)
I have a lot of work ***to be done**. (×)

(cf.) There is[are] ~ 구문의 명사를 수식하는 부정사는 능동태와 수동태 모두 가능
There are many books **to read**.
= There are many books **to be read**.

4) 형용사를 수식하는 to부정사

문장의 주어가 부정사의 의미상의 목적어이므로 능동태로 쓴다.

> The work is difficult **to do**. (○)
> The work is difficult ***to be done**. (×)

5) 앞의 명사를 수식하는 to부정사

보어 등 문미의 명사를 수식하는 경우, 수식되는 명사가 행위의 주체이면 능동태, 대상이면 수동태를 쓴다.

> She is the last person **to betray** others.
> = She is the last person that will betray others.
> "Macbeth" was the best play **to be performed** that year.
> = "Macbeth" was the best play that was performed that year.

6) 능동형으로 수동의 뜻을 나타내는 to부정사

> He is **to blame** for his unethical behavior. (= to be blamed)
> This house is **to let**. (= to be let)

9. 부정사의 부정

부정어를 to부정사 바로 앞에 둔다.

> He ran in order **not to miss** the train.
> I told him **not to be** late for work.
> I decided **not to marry** her.

10. 대부정사

부정사의 반복을 피하기 위해 to만 쓰는 것을 의미한다.

> You may call me if you'd like **to**. (= to call me)
> I asked her to play the violin, but she did not want **to**. (= to play the violin)

11. 분리부정사

to부정사가 부사에 의해 분리되는 것으로, 부정사의 의미를 보다 명확하게 하기 위해 사용된다.

He failed **to entirely understand** the subject. <부분부정>

(cf.) He entirely failed to understand the subject. 〈전체부정〉

12. 독립부정사

to be frank with you 솔직히 말하면
to be sure 확실히(= for sure)
to begin with 우선, 먼저(= first of all, in the first place)
to do him justice 공정하게 말하자면
to make matters worse 설상가상으로(= what is worse)
to tell the truth 사실을 말하자면
to make a long story short 간단히 말하면(= in short)
so to speak 말하자면(= as it were)
strange to say 이상한 얘기지만
not to speak of ~은 말할 것도 없이(= to say nothing of, not to mention, let alone)

13. to부정사의 관용표현

1) in order to부정사 = so as to부정사 ~하기 위하여

She works hard **in order to succeed**.
= She works hard **so as to succeed**.
= She works hard **so that** she **may[can] succeed**.
= She works hard **in order that** she **may[can] succeed**.

2) in order not to부정사 = so as not to부정사 ~하지 않기 위하여

She listened attentively **in order not to miss** a single word.
= She listened attentively **so as not to miss** a single word.
= She listened attentively **so that** she **might not miss** a single word.
= She listened attentively **lest** she **should miss** a single word.
= She listened attentively **for fear that** she **should miss** a single word.

3) so 형용사/부사 as to부정사 ~할 만큼 …하다, ~해서 …하다

He got up **so** early **as to be** in time for the train.
= He got up **so** early **that** he was in time for the train.

4) too ~ to부정사 너무 ~해서 …할 수 없다

These boxes are **too** heavy for me **to move**.
= These boxes are **so** heavy **that** I **cannot move** them.

5) 형용사/부사 enough to부정사 ~할 만큼 …하다

This computer is small **enough** for me **to carry**.
= This computer is **so** small **that** I can carry it.

6) know better than to부정사 ~할 정도로 어리석지는 않다

He **knows better than to judge** by appearances.

14. 원형부정사

1) 지각동사 + 목적어 + 원형부정사

I *saw* him **cross** the road.
I have never *heard* her **use** bad language.
She *noticed* the lusty man with a black cap **follow** her.

2) 사역동사 + 목적어 + 원형부정사

I *made* him **clean** my room.
I always *let* my children **do** what they want to.
I *had* the tailor **make** my dress.
Exercise will *help* you (to) **keep** your body healthy.

3) 일반동사 뒤에 원형부정사가 오는 경우

She **made believe** not to hear me.
We had to **make do with** a quick snack.
He didn't **let go of** his anger easily.

4) 주어가 All, What, The only thing 등으로 시작하여 do 동사로 끝난 경우, be동사의 보어 자리에 원형부정사를 쓸 수 있다.

All he did was **open** the door.
What we have got to do first is **go** and **see** him.
The only thing I want to do is **sleep** enough.

5) 두 개의 부정사가 and, or, except, but, than, as, like 등과 연결될 때 뒤에 오는 부정사는 원형부정사를 사용한다.

I'd like *to lie* down and **go** to sleep.
Do you want *to have* lunch now or **wait** until later?

동명사(Gerund)

1. 동명사의 역할

동명사는 명사의 속성과 동사의 속성을 함께 가지고 있다.

1) 명사적 기능

① 주어

Rising early is good for the health.
Listening to music is one of his greatest satisfactions.
Understanding each other's differences is very important.

② 보어

His hobby is **collecting** stamps.
One of her good habits is **taking** notes.

③ 목적어

She finished **writing** a letter. <타동사의 목적어>
He wasn't interested in **learning** to play the violin. <전치사의 목적어>

(cf.) 동명사가 완전히 명사화되어 관사나 형용사의 수식을 받으면 '전치사 + 명사'를 수반한다.

A good **understanding** *of grammar* is essential for good writing.

2) 동사적 기능

목적어나 보어를 취할 수 있고 부사의 수식을 받는다.

> He enjoyed **playing** *soccer* with my classmates.
> She is ashamed of **being** *ignorant*.
> We can't succeed without **working** *hard*.

2. 동명사의 의미상의 주어

1) 의미상의 주어를 명시하는 경우

① 문장의 주어와 다른 경우에 표시하며, 소유격을 쓰는 것이 원칙이다.

> *We* certainly appreciate **your letting** us stay with you.
> *Her father* was proud of **her marrying** a soldier.
> Do *you* mind **my making** a suggestion?

② 무생물이나 부정대명사의 경우에는 목적격을 쓴다.

> I don't like ***anyone's meddling** in my affair. (×)
> I don't like **anyone meddling** in my affair. (○)
> They were glad of **the examination being** over.
> She insists on **someone helping** her do it.

(cf.) 동명사의 생략된 의미상 주어는 주절의 주어와 일치해야 한다.
> On **hearing** the news, **my mind* was changed. (×)
> On **hearing** the news, *I* changed my mind. (○)

2) 의미상의 주어를 명시하지 않는 경우

① 일반주어인 경우

> **Studying** English is no easy task.
> **Seeing** is believing.

② 문장의 주어와 일치하거나 문장의 목적어와 일치하는 경우

> *He* insists on **attending** the party. <의미상의 주어가 문장의 주어와 일치>
> I don't blame *you* for **leaving** him. <의미상의 주어가 문장의 목적어와 일치>

3. 동명사의 시제

1) 단순동명사: 동사원형 + ing

본동사와 동일시제 혹은 미래의 행위를 나타낸다.

> He *is* ashamed of **being** poor.
> = He *is* ashamed that he *is* poor.
> He *was* ashamed of **being** poor.
> = He *was* ashamed that he *was* poor.
> I *am* sure of his **passing** the exam.
> = I *am* sure that he *will pass* the exam.
> I *was* sure of his **passing** the exam.
> = I *was* sure that he *would pass* the exam.

2) 완료동명사: having p.p.

본동사보다 한 시제 앞선 시제를 나타낸다.

> He *is* ashamed of **having been** poor.
> = He *is* ashamed that he *was(has been)* poor.
> He *was* ashamed of **having been** poor.
> = He *was* ashamed that he *had been* poor.

(cf.) remember, forget, regret 뒤에는 단순 동명사가 완료 동명사의 역할을 대신할 수 있다.

> I *remember* **seeing** her.
> = I *remember* that I *saw* her.
> She *regrets* **telling** him the story.
> = She *regrets* that she *told* him the story.

4. 동명사의 태

1) 능동형과 수동형

① 능동형
   동명사의 의미상 주어가 행위의 주체

> The director was famous for **treating** actors badly. <단순>
> She denied **having heard** the news. <완료>

제7강 동명사

② 수동형
   동명사의 의미상 주어가 행위의 대상

> I don't like **being asked** to make a speech. <단순>
> I never heard of such a thing **having been done**. <완료>

2) 능동형으로 수동의 의미를 나타내는 경우

want/ need/ deserve/ require/ be worth + ~ing

> His house **needs[wants] painting**.
> = His house needs[wants] to be painted.
> This novel **is worth reading** once.
> = This novel is worthy of reading once.
> = This novel is worthy to be read once.
> = It is worth while to read this novel once.

5. 동명사의 부정

부정어를 동명사 바로 앞에 둔다.

> There is a chance of his **coming** *not. (×)
> There is a chance of *not his **coming**. (×)
> There is a chance of his **not coming**. (○)
> I was sorry for **not having kept** the promise.
> She was ashamed of **never having been** in time for school.

6. '전치사 to + ~ing' 구문

1) be used[accustomed] to ~ing ~에 익숙하다

> He **is used to playing** the piano in front of big crowds.

(cf.) be used to + 동사원형 ~하는 데 사용되다
   used to + 동사원형 ~하곤 했다
   These brushes **are used to paint** big pictures.
   I **used to get** up early in the morning.

2) look forward to ~ing ~을 기대하다, 고대하다

We are **looking forward to hearing** from you.

3) object to ~ing ~에 반대하다(= be opposed to ~ing)

I **object to working** on Sundays.

4) contribute to ~ing ~에 공헌하다

Everyone on the team **contributed to winning** the game.

5) devote[dedicate/ commit] oneself to ~ing ~에 전념하다

She **devoted herself to helping** the poor.

6) with a view to ~ing ~할 목적으로

She went abroad **with a view to studying** music.

7) what do you say to ~ing ~하는 게 어떻습니까?

What do you say to eating out tonight?
= How about eating out tonight?

8) come close to ~ing 하마터면 ~할 뻔하다

He **came close to losing** his wife after a car accident.

9) confess to ~ing ~을 자백하다

He **confessed to having** stolen the jewelry.

10) when it comes to ~ing ~에 관한 한, ~에 관해서라면

When it comes to playing the piano, you can't beat Sharon.

제7강 동명사

11) take to ~ing ~을 매우 좋아하게 되다, ~을 탐닉하다

He **took to skiing** from his first day on the slopes.

12) lead to ~ing ~을 초래하다

His diligence **led to succeeding** in his life.

7. 동명사의 관용표현

1) There is no ~ing ~하는 것은 불가능하다, ~할 수 없다

   There is no knowing what may happen tomorrow.
   = It is impossible to know what may happen tomorrow.
   = We cannot know what may happen tomorrow.

2) It is no use[good] ~ing ~해도 소용없다

   It is no use[good] trying to persuade him.
   = It is of no use to try to persuade him.

3) cannot help ~ing ~하지 않을 수 없다

   I **cannot help admiring** his courage.
   = I cannot but admire his courage.
   = I have no choice but to admire his courage.

4) feel like ~ing ~하고 싶은 생각이 들다

   I **feel like going** to the movies tonight.

5) It goes without saying that ~은 두말할 필요도 없다

   It goes without saying that health is above wealth.
   = It is needless to say that health is above wealth.

6) never[not] ~ without ···ing ~하기만 하면 반드시 ···하다

> They **never** meet **without quarreling**.
> = Whenever they meet, they quarrel.

7) far from ~ing 결코 ~이 아닌, ~하기는커녕

> We are **far from agreeing** with his opinions.
> **Far from blaming** him, I thank him for his conduct.

8) of one's own ~ing 자신이 직접 ~한

> This is the tree **of his own planting**.

9) make a point of ~ing ~을 규칙으로 하다, 반드시 ~하다

> I **make a point of taking** a walk every morning.
> = I make it a rule to take a walk every morning.

10) be on the point[brink] of ~ing 막 ~하려는 참이다

> He **was on the point of breathing** his last breath.
> = He was about to breathe his last breath.

11) on[upon] ~ing ~하자마자

> **On receiving** the letter, she turned pale.
> = As soon as she received the letter, she turned pale.

12) be busy (in) ~ing ~하느라고 바쁘다

> She **was busy (in) taking** care of her patients.

13) have difficulty[trouble/ a hard time] + (in) ~ing
~하는 데 곤란[어려움]을 겪다

> Many foreign students **have difficulty (in) learning** the Korean language.

14) spend + 시간, 돈 + (in) ~ing ~하는 데 시간[돈]을 쓰다

> He **spends his spare time (in) drawing** pictures.

15) without so much as ~ing ~조차도 없이

> He left **without so much as saying** good-bye.

16) go ~ing ~하러 가다

> Let's **go shopping** at a department store tomorrow.

17) be worth ~ing ~할 가치가 있다

> The stock **is worth buying**.
> = The stock is worthy of buying.
> = The stock is worthy to be bought.
> = It is worth while to buy the stock.

분사(Participle)

1. 분사에 내포된 의미

자동사의 현재분사는 진행을 의미하고 과거분사는 완료를 의미한다.
타동사의 현재분사는 능동을 의미하고 과거분사는 수동을 의미한다.

falling leaves <진행의 의미>
fallen leaves <완료의 의미>
an **exciting** scene <능동의 의미>
the **excited** crowd <수동의 의미>

2. 분사의 용법

1) 한정적 용법

분사 단독으로 명사를 수식하는 경우에는 수식하는 명사 앞에 놓인다. 여기에 다른 부사, 부사구, 목적어, 보어 따위가 붙어서 두 단어 이상이 될 때에는 수식하는 명사 뒤에 놓인다.

a **sleeping** baby <전치수식>
a **wounded** soldier <전치수식>
a baby **sleeping** *in the cradle* <수식어구 동반, 후치수식>
a soldier **wounded** *in the back* <수식어구 동반, 후치수식>

(cf.) 단독분사라도 다음의 경우에는 후치 수식한다.
① 일시적, 동사적 속성을 나타내는 경우
the people **attending**
the problems **discussed**
② 대명사를 수식하는 경우
those **invited**

2) 서술적 용법

분사가 동사의 보어로서 쓰이는 용법으로, 주격 보어 및 목적격 보어의 두 가지로 사용된다.

① 주격 보어

The students sat **surrounding** their teacher.
The teacher sat **surrounded** by the students.

② 목적격 보어

I found her **weeping** in the room.
I found her **killed** in the room.

3. 분사의 명사화

'the + 형용사/분사'는 '복수[단수]명사, 추상명사'를 나타낸다.

1) 복수보통명사를 나타내는 경우

the poor, the rich, the wounded, the injured, the disabled, the employed, the unemployed 등

The government distributes free food to **the poor**.
The killed and **the wounded** lay on the battle-field.

2) 단수보통명사를 나타내는 경우

the accused, the deceased, the assured, the condemned 등

The accused was released on bail.
The deceased was a great scholar.

3) 추상명사를 나타내는 경우: 단수 취급

the unknown, the unexpected, the untouched, the true, the good 등

The known is limited while **the unknown** is an infinity.
She has an eye for **the beautiful**. (심미안이 있다)

4. 현재분사 + 명사 vs. 동명사 + 명사

'현재분사 + 명사'는 명사의 행위와 동작을 나타내고, '동명사 + 명사'는 명사의 용도와 목적을 표현한다.

a **sleeping** baby = a baby who is sleeping 잠자고 있는 아기 <분사>
a **sleeping** car = a car for sleeping 잠을 자기 위한 차(= 침대차) <동명사>
smoking people = people who smoke 흡연자 <분사>
a **smoking** area = an area for smoking 흡연구역 <동명사>

5. 감정 타동사의 분사

감정을 유발하는 경우에는 현재분사를 쓰고, 감정을 느끼게 되는 경우에는 과거분사를 쓴다.

놀라게 하다: surprise, amaze, astonish, astound, frighten, alarm
기쁘게 하다, 만족시키다: amuse, delight, please, satisfy
실망시키다: disappoint, discourage, frustrate
당황하게 하다: embarrass, bewilder, confuse, puzzle, perplex, baffle
흥미를 유발하다: interest, intrigue
지루하게 하다: bore   흥분하게 하다: excite
지치게 하다: tire, exhaust   우울하게 하다: depress

The news was **surprising**.
We were **surprised** at the news.
The play was **boring**.
The play made us **bored**.

(cf.) He is a very **boring** person. 〈사람이 지루함을 유발〉

6. 분사 형용사

동사적 성질이 사라져서 온전히 형용사처럼 쓰이는 분사를 의미한다.

1) 현재분사형 형용사

missing 실종된
fascinating 멋진, 매력적인
demanding 요구가 지나친, 까다로운
lasting 지속적인
striking 두드러진
appetizing 식욕을 돋우는
pressing 절박한, 긴급한

becoming 잘 어울리는
promising 유망한
whopping 엄청난
overwhelming 압도적인
engaging 매력적인
enlightening 계몽적인
trying 견디기 어려운, 힘든, 화나는

The police are searching for the **missing** child.
<missed를 쓰지 않도록 유의>
I enclosed a list of my most **pressing** problems.

2) 과거분사형 형용사

crowded 붐비는, 만원의
qualified 자격 있는
engaged 바쁜
prejudiced/ biased 편견을 가진
sophisticated 복잡한, 정교한, 세련된
celebrated/ distinguished/ noted 유명한

complicated 복잡한
disappointed 실망한, 기대가 어긋난
established 확립된, 기성의
unrestrained 억제되지 않은, 무제한의

The room was **crowded** with furniture.
I don't like to see students **disappointed**.
This is an **established** fact.
Medical techniques are becoming more **sophisticated**.

7. 유사분사

명사에 과거분사형 접미사인 '-ed'를 붙여 '~한', '~을 가진'이란 의미의 형용사처럼 쓴다. 흔히 부사나 형용사가 하이픈과 함께 앞에 온다.

```
talented 재주 있는              wooden 나무로 만든
moneyed 부유한                  warm-hearted 마음이 따뜻한
red-feathered 깃털이 붉은       blue-eyed 파란 눈을 가진
red-haired 빨간 머리를 가진     bad-tempered 성미가 까다로운
```

8. 복합분사

명사, 형용사, 부사가 하이픈을 통해 분사와 결합하여 형용사처럼 쓰인다. 복합분사도 수식되는 명사가 주체이면 -ing, 대상이면 p.p.이다.

English-speaking people = people who speak English
money-oriented society = society which is oriented by money

1) 명사 + 현재분사

```
English-speaking 영어를 말하는        decision-making 결정을 내리는
peace-loving 평화를 사랑하는          war-hating 전쟁을 싫어하는
meat-eating 육식을 하는               pain-killing 통증을 없애는
ice-breaking 서먹한 분위기를 깨는     time-consuming 시간이 걸리는
thought-provoking 시사하는 바가 있는  mouth-watering 군침이 도는
air-polluting 대기를 오염시키는
```

2) 명사 + 과거분사

```
man-made 사람이 만든              male-dominated 남성주도형의
money-oriented 돈이 지배하는      knife-cut 칼에 베인
horse-drawn 말이 끄는             poverty-stricken 가난에 시달리는
```

3) 형용사 + 현재분사

good-looking 잘 생긴
bitter-tasting 쓴 맛이 나는
funny-sounding 재밌게 들리는
bad-smelling 나쁜 냄새가 나는

4) 형용사 + 과거분사

ready-made 준비된 상태로 만들어진
innocent-proved 무죄로 밝혀진
old-fashioned 구식의
guilty-found 유죄로 판명된
short-sighted 근시의

5) 부사 + 현재분사

long-lasting 오래 지속되는
hard-working 열심히 일하는
fast-walking 빨리 걷는
never-ending 끝나지 않는, 영원한
early-rising 일찍 일어나는
ever-lasting 영원한, 끊임없는

6) 부사+과거분사

newly-born 새로[갓] 태어난
well-known 잘 알려진
widely-read 널리 읽히는
newly-married 신혼의
well-made 잘 만들어진

9. 분사구문의 형태와 종류

'접속사+주어+동사' 형태의 부사절을 '분사를 이용한 구의 형태'로 줄인 것으로, 문두, 문중, 문미에 모두 올 수 있다.

> **When I arrived** in Tokyo, I contacted him.
> → **Arriving** in Tokyo, I contacted him.
> **As the dog barked** me, I ran away.
> → **The dog barking** me, I ran away.
> **Smiling brightly**, he offered me a chair. <문두>
> The lady, **smiling brightly**, handed me a photo. <문중>
> The man extended his hand, **smiling brightly**. <문미>

1) 시간 when, while, as, after (~할 때)

> **Walking** along the street, I met an old friend of mine.
> = **When I was walking** along the street, I met an old friend of mine.

2) 이유 as, because, since (~이므로)

> **There being** no bus on the street, she had to go home on foot.
> = **As there was** no bus on the street, she had to go home on foot.

3) 조건 if (~한다면)

> **Turning** to the left, you will find the school.
> = **If you turn** to the left, you will find the school.

4) 양보 though, although, even if (비록 ~이지만)

> **Trying** our best, we lost the game.
> = **Although we tried** our best, we lost the game.

5) 연속동작 and (그리고 ~하다)

> The train leaves at six, **arriving** at Busan at noon.
> = The train leaves at six, **and it arrives** at Busan at noon.

6) 동시동작 while, as (~하면서)

Smiling brightly, he waved his hand.
= **While he smiled** brightly, he waved his hand.
Singing and dancing together, we had a good time.
= **As we sang and danced** together, we had a good time.

7) 결과 and, so that (그 결과 ~하다)

It rained for two weeks on end, **completely ruining** our holiday.
= It rained for two weeks on end, **and(= so that) it completely ruined** our holiday.

10. 분사구문의 시제

1) 단순분사구문

주절의 시제와 분사구문의 시제가 일치하는 경우 단순분사구문을 쓴다.

Living in a remote village, I rarely have visitors.
= As I *live* in a remote village, I rarely *have* visitors.
Living in a remote village, I rarely had visitors.
= As I *lived* in a remote village, I rarely *had* visitors.

2) 완료분사구문

주절의 시제보다 분사구문의 시제가 하나 앞설 때 완료분사구문(having p.p.)을 쓴다.

Having lived in America, he is proficient in English.
= As he *lived(has lived)* in America, he *is* proficient in English.
Having lived in America, he was proficient in English.
= As he *had lived* in America, he *was* proficient in English.

11. 분사구문의 태

주절의 주어가 행위의 주체이면 능동분사구문, 행위의 대상이면 수동분사구문이 된다.

> Romeo, ***believed** that Juliet was dead, decided to kill himself. (×)
> Romeo, **believing** that Juliet was dead, decided to kill himself. (○)
> The dog, ***training** carefully, will make a faithful servant. (×)
> The dog, **trained** carefully, will make a faithful servant. (○)

(cf.) 수동분사구문 앞의 being, having been은 생략할 수 있다.
> **(Being) Compared** with other children of the same age, Robert is very tall.
> **(Having been) Founded** in 1906, the company has a reputation for tradition.

(cf.) 형용사 앞의 being도 생략이 가능하다.
> **(Being) Afraid** of being punished, he did not tell the truth.
> Supper **(being) ready**, we went into the dining room.

12. 분사구문의 부정

분사구문을 부정할 경우 부정어를 분사 앞에 둔다.

> *****Having never talked** with him, I don't know where he is from. (×)
> **Never having talked** with him, I don't know where he is from. (○)
> I'm afraid of going abroad, *****being not able** to speak English. (×)
> I'm afraid of going abroad, **not being able** to speak English. (○)

13. 접속사 + 분사구문

분사구문의 의미를 보다 명확히 하기 위해 분사구문 앞에 시간, 조건, 양보 등의 접속사를 남겨 놓을 수도 있다.

> **When telephoning** from abroad, dial 822, not 8202.
> **After graduating** from college, Mr. Kim went to America.
> **If used** wisely, leisure promotes health and happiness.
> Blair, **although born** in Kentucky, lived in Missouri.

(cf.) 분사구문의 주어가 주절의 주어와 다른 경우에는 접속사를 남겨놓을 수 없다.
*****When her husband dying**, *she* received $1 billion in insurance. (×)
When *her husband* died, *she* received $1 billion in insurance. (○)

14. 독립분사구문

1) 분사구문의 의미상 주어와 주절의 주어는 일치해야 한다.

Returning to my apartment, **the window* was open. (×)
Returning to my apartment, *I* found the window open. (○)
= When I returned to my apartment, the window was open.
Written in haste, *I* found many misprints in the book. (×)
Written in haste, *the book* has many misprints. (○)
= As it was written in haste, the book has many misprints.

2) 독립분사구문

분사구문의 의미상 주어가 주절의 주어와 일치하지 않을 경우, 분사구문의 주어를 명시해야 한다.

As *my mother* was sick, *I* took her to the hospital.
→ **My mother being sick**, *I* took her to the hospital.
As *an eye was* bandaged, *I* could not write properly.
→ **An eye bandaged**, I could not write properly.
As *it* was a fine day, *we* went hiking.
→ **It being** a fine day, *we* went hiking. <비인칭 주어 it>
As *there* was no evidence against him, *he* was released.
→ **There being** no evidence against him, *he* was released. <유도부사 there>

15. 무인칭 독립분사구문

말하는 이의 의견이나 판단을 나타내는 경우, 주어의 일치 여부와 상관없이 분사구문의 의미상 주어 I, We 등을 생략하는데, 이를 무인칭 독립분사구문이라 한다.

generally speaking 일반적으로 말하면
strictly speaking 엄격하게 말하면
frankly speaking 솔직하게 말하면
judging from ~으로 판단컨대
taking ~ into consideration ~을 고려하면, ~을 고려해 보았을 때
granting[granted] that ~이라 할지라도
seeing (that) ~이므로, ~때문에
compared with[to] ~와 비교해서
weather permitting 날씨가 좋으면, 날씨가 허락한다면
other things being equal 다른 조건이 같다면
all things considered 모든 사실을 고려해 본다면

Generally speaking, women live longer than men.
Strictly speaking, she is not a superstar.
Judging from his expression, he is in a bad mood.
Taking everything **into consideration**, you ought to go home and get some rest.
Compared with his brother, he is not so intelligent.
We'll go on a picnic, **weather permitting**.

16. with 분사구문

부대상황이나 이유를 나타내는 독립분사구문 앞에 전치사 with를 놓을 수 있다. 이때 목적어와 이하 요소들은 주술 관계에 있다.

1) with + 목적어 + 현재분사

> He sat silently, and the cat was dozing at his feet.
> = He sat silently, the cat dozing at his feet.
> = He sat silently, **with the cat dozing** at his feet.
> The dog barked at me **with its tail wagging**.
> My mother spoke **with tears falling** down her cheeks.

2) with + 목적어 + 과거분사

> He stood there, and he closed his eyes.
> = He stood there, closing his eyes.
> = He stood there, his eyes (being) closed (by him).
> = He stood there, **with his eyes closed**.
> He returned **with his leg injured**.
> He was standing by the door **with his arms folded**.

3) with + 목적어 + 형용사

> Don't speak **with your mouth full**.
> She was sleeping **with his mouth open**.

4) with + 목적어 + 부사(구)

> I shall be lonely **with you away**.
> He stood **with his hat in hand**.
> He sleeps upside down **with his feet on the pillow**.
> Laura sat at the back of the class **with her hat on**.

17. 분사형 전치사

> barring ~을 제외하고는, ~이 없다면
> concerning/ regarding ~에 관하여
> considering ~을 고려해 볼 때 <흔히 that절을 수반>
> given ~이 주어지면, ~을 고려해 볼 때 <종종 that절을 수반>
> depending on ~에 따라, ~에 좌우되어
> following ~한 후에
> including ~을 포함하여
> notwithstanding ~에도 불구하고
> pending ~하는 동안, ~하는 중
> regarding ~에 관하여

Considering his age, he looks young.
Following the meeting, tea will be served.
The band played many songs, **including** some of my favorites.
Notwithstanding his offer, we left the company.
He looks young **considering (that)** he is so old.
Given good health, one can achieve anything.
= **Given that** one is in good health, one can achieve anything.

18. 분사구문의 강조

분사구문을 강조하는 어구는 주로 이유를 나타내는 분사구문에 쓰이며, 접속사 as를 써서 표현한다. '사실[정말] ~하기 때문에'라는 의미를 나타낸다.

1) 현재분사 + as + 주어 + do동사

Standing as it does on the hill, my house commands a fine view.
Living as I do, so remote from towns, I rarely have visitors.

2) 과거분사 + as + 주어 + be동사

Written as it is in plain English, the book is easy to understand.
Hidden as it was, the temple was difficult to find.

접속사(Conjunction)

1. 등위접속사

1) and: 열거, 인과

I want a pen **and** a piece of paper.
I missed supper **and** I'm starving.

2) but(= yet): 대조, 역접, 양보

He is rich, **but** (he is) not happy.
Excuse me, **but** could you tell me the time?

3) or: 선택, 동격

Would you like coffee **or** tea?
She was born in Saigon, **or** Ho Chi Minh City as it is now called.

4) for: (부가적인) 이유

It is morning, **for** the birds are singing.
I went to bed early, **for** I was tired.

(cf.) because, as, since와 달리, for가 이끄는 절은 주절 앞에 쓰지 못한다.
　***For** he can speak English well, he is very proud. (×)
　He is very proud, **for** he can speak English well. (○)

5) so: 결과

> The audience was seated, and **so** the speech began.
> He didn't want to make her unhappy, **so** he told a white lie.

6) nor: ~도 또한 …않다

> He is not rich, **nor** does he want to be.
> You don't like it, **nor** do I.

(cf.) He cannot *read* **or** *write*. 〈단어, 구 연결: or〉
　　　He can *neither* read **nor** write. 〈neither 뒤: 항상 nor〉

(cf.) nor vs. neither
　　　nor는 접속사이므로 두 문장의 연결에 쓰이며, neither 부사이므로 완전히
　　　끝난 문장 뒤 혹은 접속사와 함께 쓴다.
　　　I don't know, **nor** do I care.
　　　= I don't know, **and neither** do I care.
　　　= I don't know, **and** I don't care, **either**.
　　　= I don't know. **Neither** do I care.

2. 명령문 + and/ or

1) 명령문(또는 must 계열 구문) + and ~해라, 그러면 …할 것이다

> *Work hard*, **and** you will succeed.
> *You must work hard*, **and** you will succeed.
> *One more mistake*, **and** you'll be fired.

2) 명령문(또는 must 계열 구문) + or ~해라, 그렇지 않으면 …할 것이다

> *Hurry up*, **or** you will miss the train.
> *You must hurry up*, **or** you will miss the train.
> *Wear your coat*, **or** you'll catch cold.

3. 등위상관접속사

1) both A and B A와 B 둘 다
   = at once A and B
   = A and B alike
   = A and B as well

   He has **both** experience **and** scholarship.
   = He has **at once** experience **and** scholarship.
   = He has experience **and** scholarship **as well**.

2) either A or B A 또는 B, A와 B 둘 중의 하나

   You are **either** guilty **or** innocent.

3) neither A nor B A도 B도 아닌, A와 B 둘 다 아닌

   I **neither** smoke **nor** drink.

4) not only A but (also) B A뿐만 아니라 B도
   = not only A but B as well
   = B as well as A

   He plays **not only** the piano, **but (also)** the violin.
   = He plays **not only** the piano, **but** the violin **as well**.
   = He plays the violin **as well as** the piano.

   (cf.) 강조를 위해 not only가 문두에 올 경우 뒤에 이어지는 주어와 동사가 도치된다.
   He **not only** heard it **but** he **also** saw it.
   → **Not only** *did he hear* it **but** he **also** saw it.

5) not A but B A가 아니라 B
   = B, (and) not A

   This is **not** my book **but** his.
   = This is his book, **(and) not** mine.

6) whether A or B A인지, B인지; A이든 B이든

I don't know **whether** he is at home **or** at the office.
Whether sick **or** well, he is always cheerful.

7) between A and B A와 B 사이에

We traveled **between** Seoul **and** Busan by railroad.

4. 접속부사

1) 접속부사의 종류

> 역접, 대조: however, though 그러나
> 인과: therefore, thus, hence, accordingly, consequently 그래서, 그러므로
> 부가: besides, moreover, furthermore 게다가, 더욱이
> 조건부정: otherwise 그렇지 않으면
> 양보: nevertheless, nonetheless 그럼에도 불구하고

I think; **therefore** I am.
I didn't feel like going there. Later, **however**, I decided to go.
The order must be delivered by Tuesday; **otherwise** we will have to look for another supplier.

2) 접속부사는 부사이므로 두 문장을 연결할 수 없으며, 세미콜론(;)과 함께 쓰거나 문장이 끝난 다음에 써야 한다. 문두뿐만 아니라, 문미나 문중에도 올 수 있다.

I am not rich, **but** I don't want your money.
= I am not rich. **However**, I don't want your money. <문두>
= I am not rich. I don't, **however**, want your money. <문중>
= I am not rich. I don't want your money, **however**. <문미>
= I am not rich; **however**, I don't want your money. <세미콜론 뒤>

5. that절

1) 주어

That he is honest is true. <동사는 단수 취급>
= **It** is true **that** he is honest. <가주어-진주어 구문>

2) 보어

The fact is **that** he is honest.

(cf.) 주어가 the reason일 경우 보어에 because절이 아닌 that절을 쓰는 것이 원칙이다.
The **reason** why I'm late is ***because** I missed the bus. (×)
The **reason** why I'm late is **that** I missed the bus. (○)

3) 목적어

I know **(that)** he is honest.
I think **(that)** health is essential to happiness.

(cf.) that절은 전치사의 목적어로 쓰일 수 없지만, 예외적으로 in과 except는 that절을 목적어로 취할 수 있다.

· in that ~라는 점에서, ~ 때문에
  Men differ from brutes **in that** they can think and speak.

· except[but] that ~라는 점을 제외하면
  She knows nothing about the story **except that** it is very long.

4) 동격

The news **that** he married is true.
The fact **that** he paid his debt proves his honesty.

5) 감정과 확신의 형용사 뒤에 이어지는 that절

I am **certain[sure/ confident/ convinced] that** you will succeed.
I am **pleased[glad] that** you have come.
I am **angry[sorry] that** she didn't come.
I am **afraid that** it will rain tomorrow.

6. whether/ if절

불확실, 의문의 뜻이 있는 경우에는 whether, if가 명사절을 이끈다.

1) 타동사의 목적어, 부정의 확신 형용사 뒤에는 whether, if 둘 다 가능하다.

He asked **whether/ if** I knew Chinese.
He wasn't sure **whether/ if** he could come.

(cf.) 종속절이 부정문일 때는 원칙적으로 if만 가능하다.
I don't care **if** it doesn't rain. 〈whether 불가〉

2) whether만 쓸 수 있는 경우

① 주어절

Whether she likes the present is not clear to me.
Whether Tom likes Mary (or not) is not clear.

② 보어절

The question is **whether** she agrees to the plan or not.

③ 동격절

There is a question **whether** his act was accidental or intentional.

④ 양보의 부사절

Whether you see her or not, phone me later.

⑤ 전치사 뒤

It depends on **whether** they will support us.
Do you worry about **whether** your child is happy?

⑥ to부정사 앞

The question is **whether** to go or stay.

⑦ or not 수반시

> I don't know **whether** it is feasible **or not**.
> = I don't know **whether or not** it is feasible.

(cf.) 감정 형용사 + if/ whether절 불가
> She is afraid/ fearful ***if*** he won't believe her story. (×)
> She is afraid/ fearful **that** he won't believe her story. (○)

7. 의문사절(간접의문문)

1) 의문사절은 명사절로서 문장의 주어, 목적어, 보어, 전치사의 목적어 역할을 한다.

> **When she will arrive here** is not known. <주어>
> I know **where she lives**. <목적어>
> She is kind to everyone. That's **why everybody likes her**. <보어>
> We are talking about **how we will go to Busan**. <전치사의 목적어>

2) '의문사 + 주어 + 동사'의 어순을 따른다.

> I wondered **when you'd show up**.
> Do you know **where he is from**?

(cf.) 의문사가 주어인 경우: 의문사 + 동사
> Do you know **who wrote** our Declaration of Independence?

3) 주절에 인식 동사 think, believe, imagine, suppose, say 등이 있는 의문문에서는 의문사가 문두로 간다. know는 여기에 해당되지 않음에 유의한다.

> Do you *think* ***who*** wrote the novel? (×)
> **Who** do you *think* wrote the novel? (○)

(cf.) Do you *know* **who** wrote the novel?

4) 의문대명사 + 불완전한 절

I don't know **who she is**.
I don't know **what she wants**.
I don't know **which she will choose**.

5) 의문부사 + 완전한 절

I don't know **when she will come back**.
I don't know **where she lives**.
I don't know **why she didn't come**.
I don't know **how she made it**.

(cf.) how + 형용사/부사
 I don't know **how old** she is.
 I don't know **how fast** she runs.

6) 의문형용사: what + 명사/ which + 명사

I don't know **what colors** she likes best.
I don't know **which season** he likes best. <제한된 대상 중에서의 선택>

8. 시간의 부사절

1) when/ while/ as

When he comes, tell him so.
Strike the iron **while** it is hot.
He went out just **as** I came in.

2) until[till]/ before

until[till]: 행위의 지속 <~까지 계속>
before: 동작의 완료 <~까지 완료>

I will stay here **until** you come back.
I will finish the work **before** you come back.

(cf.) not A until B   B하고 나서야 비로소 A하다
    I did **not** learn Hangeul **until** I came to Korea.
    = **Not until** I came to Korea *did I learn* Hangeul. 〈주절의 주어와 동사 도치〉
    = *It* was **not until** I came to Korea *that* I learned Hangeul. 〈강조구문〉

(cf.) not A before B   채 A하기 전에 B하다
    I had **not** walked a mile **before[when]** I got tired.
    It will not be long before we *meet* again.
    〈머지않아, 시간부사절인 before 이하는 현재시제〉

3) since/ after

since: 과거부터 현재까지의 계속 <주절은 현재완료, 종속절은 과거시제>
after: 과거 또는 미래에 일어난 일 <주절은 시점에 맞추어 과거 또는 미래시제>

> I *have lived* here **since** I *was* born.
> We*'ve been* friends ever **since** we *met* at school.
> Mr. Park *went* to America **after** he *graduated* from high school last year.
> Mr. Park *will go* to America **after** he *graduates* from high school next year.

4) As soon as S + V(과거시제), S + V(과거시제) ~하자마자 …하다
= Hardly[Scarcely] + had + S + p.p. ~ when[before] + S + V(과거시제)
= No sooner + had + S + p.p. ~ than + S + V(과거시제)

> **As soon as** she *left* home it *began* to rain.
> = She *had* hardly *left* home **when/ before** it *began* to rain.
> = **Hardly** *had* she *left* home **when/ before** it *began* to rain.
> = **No sooner** *had* she *left* home **than** it *began* to rain.

5) once 일단 ~하면

> **Once** you start, you must finish it.
> **Once** you learn the basic rules, this game is easy.

6) by the time ~할 때는 이미, ~할 때쯤에는
by the time S + V(과거), S + had + p.p.
by the time S + V(현재), S + will + have + p.p.

> **By the time** the doctor *arrived*, the patient *had* already *died*.
> **By the time** you *arrive*, we *will* already *have gone*.

7) while <접속사> vs. during <전치사>

> Make hay **while** *the sun shines*.
> **During** *the 1970's*, South Korea made great economic progress.

9. 이유, 원인의 부사절

1) because

> I could not go out **because** I had caught cold.
> He was absent **because** he was ill.

(cf.) 부정문 안에서 because가 쓰인 경우 해석에 유의한다.
  Do **not** despise a man **because** he is poor.
  가난하다고 해서 사람을 멸시하지는 마라.

2) since

> **Since** he says so I shall have to believe it.
> **Since** there's no more time, we must give it up.

3) as

> **As** you are sorry I'll forgive you.
> **As** it was fine yesterday, I went fishing.

4) now that/ seeing that ~이니까, ~인 이상

> **Now that** she is gone, we miss her.
> **Seeing that** you lied to me, I can't trust you any longer.

5) in that ~라는 점에서

The plan is unrealistic **in that** it requires too much expense.

(cf.) now that이 문두, 문중에 모두 쓰이는 것과 달리, in that은 주절의 뒤에만 쓰일 수 있다.

 ***In that** it may discourage people from working harder, high income tax is bad. (×)

6) because <접속사> vs.
because of/ on account of/ owing to/ due to/ thanks to <전치사구>

Because it *rained*, we couldn't go on a picnic.
Because of *rain*, we couldn't go on a picnic.

10. 목적의 부사절

1) (so) that + S + may[can/ will] ~하기 위해
 = (in order) that + S + may

They hurried **(so) that** they **might** catch the train.
He works hard **(in order) that** he **may** support his family.

2) lest ~ (should) ~하지 않도록, ~하지 않기 위해
 = for fear (that) ~ (should)

I worked hard **lest** I **(should)** fail in the examination.
He didn't leave the house **for fear (that)** someone **(should)** recognize him.

(cf.) lest ~ should, for fear ~ should는 그 자체에 부정의 의미를 포함하고 있으므로 뒤에 부정어를 써서는 안 된다.
 Take careful of yourself **lest** you **should** *not* catch a cold. (×)

11. 결과의 부사절

1) so ~ that/ such ~ that 너무 ~해서 …하다

The problem was **so** difficult **that** I could not solve it.
He is **such** a kind boy **that** everybody likes him.
She is **so** honest a woman **that** I like her.
= She is **such** an honest woman **that** I like her.

2) so (that) 그래서 ~하다

It was too dark to go on, **so (that)** we camped there.

3) 주의해야 할 어순

① such + a(n) + 형용사 + 단수명사 + that
  so + 형용사 + a(n) + 단수명사 + that
  so + 형용사/부사 + that

It was **such a boring speech that** I fell asleep.
She was **so pretty a girl that** everybody liked her.
I was **so happy that** I was speechless.

② such + 형용사 + 복수명사/불가산명사 + that
  so + many[much/ few/ little] + 명사 + that

They were **such kind boys that** everyone liked them.
It was **such fine weather that** we went for a walk.
Jack has **so many friends that** he is always busy.

4) 결과를 나타내는 부사절의 대용어구

He is **so** rich **that** he can buy a private plane.
= He is rich **enough to** buy a private plane.
I was **so** tired **that** I could **not** take another step.
= I was **too** tired **to** take another step.

12. 조건의 부사절

1) if 만약 ~이면(= provided[providing] (that), suppose[supposing] (that))

> I would go with you **if** I could.
> I will do so **providing (that)** I am paid.
> **Suppose (that)** you were in my shoes what would you do?

2) unless ~하지 않으면(= if ~ not)

> **Unless** you tell me all about it I cannot help you.
> = **If** you **don't** tell me all about it I cannot help you.

(cf.) unless는 자체에 부정의 의미가 있으므로 뒤에 부정어가 올 수 없다.
He'll accept the job **unless** the salary is *not* too low. (×)

3) in case (that) ~에 대비하여

> I wrote down her phone number **in case** I should forget it.

4) on condition (that) ~이라는 조건으로, ~이라면

> I will undertake it **on condition that** you pay the expense.

5) so[as] long as ~하는 한, ~하기만 하면

> You may stay here **so long as** you keep quiet.

13. 양보의 부사절

1) although, though, even though, even if 비록 ~일지라도

> **Although** he is poor, he is happy.
> I'll go out **even if** it rains.

2) whereas, while ~인 반면, ~이지만

> He drives to school, **whereas** I always walk.
> **While** I admit that it is difficult, I don't think it impossible.

3) no matter + 의문사 ~일지라도(= 의문사 + ever)

> **No matter who** may come, he will be welcome.
> = **Whoever** may come, he will be welcome.
> **No matter what** you say and do, you should be sincere.
> = **Whatever** you say and do, you should be sincere.

4) no matter how 형용사/부사 아무리 ~해도

> **No matter how dry** a desert may be, it is not necessarily worthless.
> = **However dry** a desert may be, it is not necessarily worthless.
> **No matter how hard** you may try, you cannot do the work.
> = **However hard** you may try, you cannot do the work.

(cf.) 형용사·부사가 however의 바로 뒤에 온다는 점에 유의한다.
> **However** I (may) write *carefully, I sometimes make mistakes. (×)
> **However carefully** I (may) write, I sometimes make mistakes. (○)

5) whether ~ or ···

> **Whether** we win **or** lose, we must play fairly.
> **Whether** it rains **or** shines, he works hard.

6) although[though] <접속사> vs. despite[in spite of] <전치사>

> **Although** *he was wealthy*, he was not always happy.
> **Despite** *his wealth*, he was not always happy.

14. as 양보절

형용사/부사/명사 + as + S + V

Patient **as[though]** he was, he couldn't wait for 3 hours.
Child **as** he was, he was brave. <as 앞의 명사는 무관사>

15. 명령형을 이용하는 양보 표현

1) 동사원형 + 의문사 + S + may[will]

Say what you will, I will go with her.
= No matter what you may say, I will go with her.
= Whatever you may say, I will go with her.

2) 동사원형 + as + S + may[will]

Try (hard) as you may, you cannot carry the stone.
= No matter how hard you may try, you cannot carry the stone.
= However hard you may try, you cannot carry the stone.

3) Be + S(3인칭) + ever so + 형용사

Be it ever so humble, there is no place like home.
= Let it be ever so humble, there is no place like home.
= However humble it may be, there is no place like home.

16. 양태의 부사절

1) as ~하는 대로, ~하듯이

Do **as** you like.
Do to others **as** you would have them do to you.
When in Rome, do **as** the Romans do.

2) (Just) As S + V, so S + V ~하는 것처럼 그렇게 …하다

> **(Just) As** rust eats iron, **so** care eats the heart.
> **As** the bees love sweetness, **so** *do the flies love* rottenness. <도치구조>

관계사(Relative)

1. 관계대명사의 특징

1) 관계대명사는 '접속사 + 대명사'의 역할을 한다.

> He has a daughter **and she** is very beautiful.
> = He has a daughter **who** is very beautiful.

2) 관계대명사 뒤에는 불완전한 절이 온다.

> Heaven helps those **who** *they* help themselves. (×)
> Heaven helps those **who** help themselves. (○)
> The lady **whom** you met *her* is a professor of music. (×)
> The lady **whom** you met is a professor of music. (○)
> The only thing **that** I worry about *it* is dying. (×)
> The only thing **that** I worry about is dying. (○)

3) 관계대명사의 격은 관계대명사나 선행사가 관계절 내에서 어떤 역할을 하는가에 의해 결정된다.

> I thanked the woman **who** *helped* me. <helped의 주어 → 주격>
> I liked the woman **whom** *I met* at the party. <met의 목적어 → 목적격>

4) 관계대명사절의 동사의 수는 선행사에 일치시킨다.

I know *a girl* **who** *is* very pretty.
I know *many girls* **who** *are* very pretty.

2. 소유격 관계대명사

1) 선행사가 사람인 경우

whose + 무관사 명사 + 동사
whose + 무관사 명사 + 주어 + 동사

I know a girl **whose father** is a doctor.
I know a girl **whose house** they want to buy.

2) 선행사가 사물인 경우

whose + 무관사 명사
the + 명사 + of which
of which + the + 명사

Look at the mountain **whose top** is covered with snow.
= Look at the mountain **the top of which** is covered with snow.
= Look at the mountain **of which the top** is covered with snow.
= Look at the mountain, **and the top of the mountain** is covered with snow.

3. 삽입절과 관계대명사의 격

관계대명사와 동사 사이에 '주어 + 인식동사' 형태의 절이 삽입될 수 있다. 이 삽입절은 관계대명사의 격에 영향을 주지 않는다.

Tom is a boy **who** *I believe* is honest. ⟨I believe는 삽입절⟩
= Tom is a boy and I believe he is honest.

(cf.) 삽입절을 제거해 보았을 때 관계사절의 구성요소를 충족하지 못한다면 삽입절이 아니다.

Tom is a boy **whom** I believe to be honest. ⟨I believe는 삽입절이 아님⟩
= Tom is a boy and I believe him to be honest.

4. 관계대명사의 제한적 용법과 계속적 용법

1) 제한적 용법

① 관계대명사 앞에 콤마(,)가 없다.
② 모든 관계대명사에 사용이 가능하다.
③ 선행사를 한정한다.

He had two sons **who** became doctors. <두 아들 외에 다른 아들이 있을 수 있다.>
There were very few passengers **who** escaped without serious injury.
<중상을 입은 승객이 대다수다.>

2) 계속적 용법

① 관계대명사 앞에 콤마(,)가 있다.
② 관계대명사 that은 사용하지 않는다.
③ 선행사에 대한 보충, 추가적 설명을 한다.

He had two sons, **who** became doctors. <아들이 둘 뿐이다.>
There were very few passengers, **who** escaped without serious injury.
<승객이 극소수였으며, 이들은 중상을 입지 않았다.>

5. 전치사 + 관계대명사

1) '전치사 + 관계대명사' 뒤에는 완전한 절이 온다.

This is the house **in which** *Churchill was born.* (○)
This is the house ***which** Churchill was born.* (×)
The music **to which** *we listened last night* was very sweet. (○)
The music ***which** we listened last night* was very sweet. (×)

2) '전치사 + 관계대명사'의 구조에서 어떤 전치사를 쓸 것인가는 선행사의 종류, 문맥, 관용구 등을 통해 판단한다.

The city **in which** factories lie is heavily polluted. <in the city에서>
He has no means of support **on which** we depend. <depend on에서>
This is the issue **with which** we are concerned. <be concerned with에서>

제10강 관계사

3) 전치사 + 관계대명사 + to부정사

관계대명사 앞에 전치사가 있는 경우, 주어가 동일하면 관계절의 주어를 생략하고 동사를 to부정사로 바꿀 수 있다.

The children had a garden **in which** they could play.
<they = The children>
= The children had a garden **in which to play**.
= The children had a garden **to play in**. <관계대명사 생략시 전치사 후치>

6. which와 that의 유의해야 할 용법

1) 계속적 용법의 관계대명사 which는 선행사가 다양할 수 있으며, 따라서 앞 문장의 형용사 보어, 부정사, 절, 앞 문장 내용 전체 등을 선행사로 가질 수 있다.

He is *rich*, **which** I unfortunately am not. <형용사가 선행사>
He tried *to solve the problem*, **which** was impossible. <to부정사가 선행사>
She remained silent, **which** made him angry. <앞 문장 전체가 선행사>

2) 선행사가 최상급, 서수, the only, the very 등의 수식을 받거나 선행사가 부정대명사, 의문대명사일 때에는 관계대명사 that을 쓴다.

It's the best film **that** has ever been made in Korea.
He was **the first** man **that** came here.
Tom is **the only** boy **that** can speak English here.
All that glitters is not gold.
Who that has common sense can believe such a thing?

3) 관계대명사 that 앞에는 전치사와 콤마(,)를 쓸 수 없다. <계속적 용법 불가>

This is the car ***about that** I told you. (×)
This is the car **that** I told you **about**. (○)
I met a boy, ***that** told me the news. (×)
I met a boy, **who** told me the news. (○)

7. 관계대명사 what

선행사를 자체에 포함하고 있는 관계대명사로(= the thing which ~, that which ~, all that ~), 다른 관계대명사가 형용사절을 이끄는 것과 달리, what은 명사절을 이끈다.

1) 명사절을 이끄는 what

문두 또는 동사 뒤에서 주어, 목적어, 보어 등의 구실을 한다.

> **What I want** is a digital camera. <주어>
> = The thing that I want is a digital camera.
> Do you believe **what he said**? <동사의 목적어>
> Jack is not **what he was**. <보어>
> = Jack is not the man that he was.

2) 관계형용사 what

what 뒤에 명사가 오면 관계형용사로서, '(적지만) ~하는 모든 ~'의 의미를 지닌다.

what + 명사 = all the + 명사 + that

> She gave him **what (little) money** she had.
> = She gave him **all the (little) money that** she had.

3) what의 관용표현

① **what one is[was/ used to be]** 현재[과거]의 인격이나 모습
   what one has 재산
   what one does 행위, 처신

> He is not **what he used to be**.
> I respect him for **what he is**, not for **what he has**.
> It is important to communicate **what you do**.

② **A is to B what[as] C is to D** A와 B의 관계는 C와 D의 관계와 같다

> Reading **is to** the mind **what** food **is to** the body.

③ what is better[worse] (still) 더욱 좋은[나쁜] 것은

He is clever, **what is better still**, very handsome.
I lost my way, and **what was worse**, it began to rain.

④ what we[you/ they] call 소위, 이른바
  = what is called
  = so called

She is **what we call** a musical genius.

⑤ what with A and (what with) B A하기도 하고 B하기도 해서 <원인>
  what by A and (what by) B A하기도 하고 B하기도 해서 <수단>

What with the cold weather **and what with** my bad leg, I haven't been out for weeks.
What by threat **and (what by)** entreaty, he attained his goal.

⑥ what is now + 지명 현재 ~인, 오늘날의 ~인

A great civilization flourished in **what is now** *northern Peru* during the first century.

8. 관계대명사의 생략

1) 목적격 관계대명사의 생략

① 타동사의 목적어

This is the boy **(whom)** *we saw* yesterday.
The book **(which/ that)** *I was reading* yesterday was a detective story.

② 전치사의 목적어

단, 전치사가 관계대명사 앞에 있을 때는 생략할 수 없다.

> This is the doll **(which/ that)** she is fond **of**.
> = This is the doll **of which** she is fond.
> The man **(whom)** you spoke **to** yesterday is my English teacher.
> = The man **to whom** you spoke yesterday is my English teacher.
> This is the house **(which/ that)** she lives **in**.
> = This is the house **in which** she lives.

2) '주격 관계대명사 + be동사'의 생략

> She always reads magazines **(which are)** written in English.
> Do you know the name of the girl **(who is)** standing over there?

3) 주격 관계대명사의 생략

① be동사의 보어일 경우

> She is not the cheerful woman **(that)** she *was*.
> He is not the man **(that)** he *was* two years ago.

② 선행사가 there is 구문의 주어일 경우

> *There is* a woman at the door **(who)** wants to see you.

③ 선행사를 there is 구문이 수식할 경우

> She is one of the greatest poets **(that)** *there are* in the world.

9. 관계대명사의 수일치 유의사항

one of + 한정사 + 복수명사 + 관계대명사 + 복수동사
the only one of + 한정사 + 복수명사 + 관계대명사 + 단수동사

> He is one of *the persons* **who talk** big.
> He is *the only one* of the persons **who talks** big.

10. 관계대명사의 이중한정

두 개의 관계대명사가 하나의 선행사를 수식하는 경우로, '~로서 …한'으로 해석한다.

> There is no one **that** I know **who** is as wise as you.
> 내가 아는 사람으로서 당신만큼 현명한 사람은 없다.
>
> Is there any book **that** you have **which** is as interesting as this?
> 당신이 가진 것으로서 이것만큼 재미있는 책이 있습니까?

11. 유사 관계대명사

1) as

① 선행사 앞에 **such, the same, as**가 있을 경우

> Choose *such* friends **as** will benefit you.
> *As* many men **as** came were given something to eat.
> I have *the same* watch **as** you have. <동일한 종류>

(cf.) I have *the same* watch **that** you lost yesterday. 〈동일물〉

② 절 전체가 선행사인 경우

> *He is afraid of doctors*, **as** is often the case with children.
> <앞 문장 전체가 선행사>
>
> **As** might have been expected, *she failed to turn up*. <뒷 문장 전체가 선행사>

2) but(= that[who] ~ not)

선행사 앞에 no, never, scarcely, hardly 등의 부정어가 있거나 수사의문문과 함께 쓰이는 경우

> There is *no* man **but** has some faults.
> = There is no man **that** does**n't** have some faults.
> *Who is there* **but** loves his own country?

3) than

선행사 앞에 비교급이 있을 경우

> She always has *more* money **than** is necessary.
> Things went *better* **than** had been expected.

12. 복합관계대명사

'관계대명사 + ever'의 형태를 취하며, 자체에 선행사를 포함하고 있다.

1) 명사절 유도

> **Whoever** wants to come is welcome. <주어>
> = **Anyone who** wants to come is welcome.
> He always says **whatever** comes into his mind. <동사의 목적어>
> = He always says **anything that** comes into his mind.
> He makes friends easily with **whomever** he meets. <전치사의 목적어>
> = He makes friends easily with **anyone whom** he meets.

2) 양보 부사절 유도

> **Whoever** may come, he will be welcome.
> = **No matter who** may come, he will be welcome.
> **Whatever** he may say, it is true.
> = **No matter what** he may say, it is true.
> **Whichever road** you may take, you will come to the same place.
> = **No matter which road** you may take, you will come to the same place.

3) 복합관계대명사의 격

관계절 내에서의 역할에 따라 격이 결정되며, 주절의 동사나 전치사는 복합관계대명사의 격에 영향을 주지 못한다.

> I will give it to **whoever** *comes* here. <관계절 안에서 주어>
> = I will give it to **anyone who** comes here.
> I will give it to **whomever** *you like*. <관계절 안에서 목적어>
> = I will give it to **anyone whom** you like.

4) whatever(= whatsoever)가 부정어의 뒤에 오면 'at all(전혀)'의 의미를 갖는다.

There is *no* doubt **whatever**.

13. 복합관계형용사

whatever, whichever는 뒤에 명사를 수반해서 복합관계형용사로 쓸 수 있다. whatever는 선택의 폭이 제한돼 있지 않은 경우, whichever는 선택의 폭이 제한돼 있는 경우에 쓴다.

He ate **whatever food** I gave him.
= He ate any food that I gave him.
Take **whichever book** you like.
= Take any one of the books that you like.

14. 관계부사

관계부사는 '접속사 + 부사'의 역할을 하며, 앞 명사를 수식하는 형용사절을 이끈다.

1) 관계부사의 종류

This is the place **where** he lives. <장소>
= This is the place **in which** he lives.
I'll never forget the day **when** I met you for the first time. <시간>
= I'll never forget the day **on which** I met you for the first time.
Tell me the reason **why** you did it. <이유>
= Tell me the reason **for which** you did it.
He told me **how** he solved the problem. <방법>
= He told me **the way** he solved the problem.
= He told me **the way in which** he solved the problem.

(cf.) 선행사 the way와 관계부사 how는 동시에 함께 쓰지 않으며, 둘 중 하나만을 써야 한다.
　Tell me *the way how you succeeded in the exam. (×)
　Tell me the way you succeeded in the exam. (○)

= Tell me **how** you succeeded in the exam.
= Tell me **the way in which** you succeeded in the exam.

(cf.) 선행사 case, circumstance, situation, point 등은 '장소 개념'으로 해석하여 관계부사 where나 in[on] which로 받는다.

There are many *cases* **where** such a principle is not practicable.

2) 관계사 뒤의 절이 완전하면 관계부사, 불완전하면 관계대명사가 된다.

전치사 뒤에는 관계부사가 아니라 관계대명사가 온다.

This is the house ***which** I lived in my childhood. (×)
This is the house **where** I lived in my childhood. (○)
= This is the house **in which** I lived in my childhood.

3) 관계부사의 생략

where를 제외한 관계부사는 생략하거나 that으로 대신할 수 있다.

Monday is the day **(that)** people feel blue. (= when)
This is the reason **(that)** I came to see you. (= why)
That was the way **(that)** she solved the problem. (= in which)

4) 선행사의 생략

① 명사절이 되는 경우

I don't know (the time) **when** the accident happened.
The local church was (the place) **where** he was laid to rest.
This is (the reason) **why** an octopus is so flexible.

② 부사절이 되는 경우

Put it back (the place) **where** it was when you are through.

5) 계속적 용법

관계부사의 계속적 용법은 where과 when에만 쓴다.

We went to London, **where** we stayed for a week.
= We went to London, **and there** we stayed for a week.
It began to rain, **when** the phone was ringing.
= It began to rain, **and then** the phone was ringing.

15. 복합관계부사

복합관계부사는 시간, 장소의 부사절과 양보의 부사절을 이끈다.

1) 시간, 장소의 부사절인 경우

> Come to see me **whenever** you are free.
> (= at any time when)
> Plants grow **wherever** there is water.
> (= at any place where)

2) 양보 부사절인 경우

> **Whenever** you may visit him, you'll find him reading something.
> (= No matter when)
> **Wherever** you go, you will not find a better place than your home.
> (= No matter where)
> **However** hard you may try, you can't do all those things in a day.
> (= No matter how)

명사와 관사
(Noun & Article)

1. 가산명사

1) 가산명사의 단수형은 한정사 (관사, 소유격, 지시형용사 등)가 반드시 필요하다.

> I like *dog. (×)
> I like a/ the/ my/ this/ every dog. (○)

2) 가산명사의 복수형은 불특정 사물이면 무관사, 특정 사물이면 the를 붙인다.

> I like **dogs**. <불특정 대상>
> I like **the dogs** in the window. <특정 대상>

2. 불가산명사

1) 불가산명사는 부정관사를 붙이지 못하며 복수형으로 쓸 수 없다.

> I like *a beer/ beers. (×)
> We need *a furniture/ furnitures. (×)

2) 불특정 사물이면 무관사, 특정 사물이면 정관사 the를 붙인다.

> I prefer **beer** to **wine**. <일반적 총칭>
> I drank all **the beer** in the refrigerator. <특정 사물>

3) 주요 불가산명사

① 추상명사

information, evidence, advice, knowledge, news, research, weather, happiness, wealth, health 등

② 고유명사

Tom, Newton, Korea, Seoul Station, The Pacific, The White House 등

③ 물질명사

water, coffee, beer (액체)/ gold, silver (고체)/ oxygen, hydrogen (기체)/ sugar, rice, corn, sand (입자)/ paper, soap, chalk (기타) 등

④ 집합적 물질명사

furniture, equipment, bread, food, game, clothing, poetry, scenery, machinery, baggage, luggage, jewelry 등

3. 명사의 전용

불가산명사가 가산명사처럼 사용되거나 추상명사가 보통명사로 사용되는 등, 명사의 성질이 변해서 사용되는 것을 뜻한다.

1) 물질명사의 보통명사화

This is **a good wine**. <종류>
Fill **the glass** with water. <제품>
There were **two fires** last night. <사건>
They threw **some stones** at the dog. <개체>

2) 추상명사의 보통명사화

She was **a beauty** in her day. <사람>
He has done me **three kindnesses**. <행위>

3) 고유명사의 보통명사화

I wish to become **a Newton**. <~와 같은 사람>
A Smith called on me yesterday. <~라는 사람>
He bought **a Ford**. <제품>
She wants to buy **a Claude Monet**. <작품>
The Bakers are happy. <~집 사람들, 부부>

4) 보통명사의 추상명사화: the + 보통명사 = 추상명사

The pen is mightier than **the sword**.
펜(文)은 칼(武)보다 강하다.
He forgot **the judge** in **the father**.
그는 부정(父情) 때문에 판사의 직분을 망각했다.

4. 추상명사를 쓰는 관용표현

1) of + 추상명사 = 형용사

---
of importance[consequence/ moment/ account] (= important)
of value (= valuable)
of experience (= experienced)
of knowledge (= knowledgeable)
of talent (= talented)
of ability (= able)

A director must be a man **of experience**.
The size of the group is **of** considerable **importance**.
He is a man **of** great **knowledge**.

2) of 이외의 전치사 + 추상명사 = 부사

---
with ease (= easily)
with confidence (= confidently)
in safety (= safely)
by intention (= intentionally)
on occasion (= occasionally)
with accuracy (= accurately)
with kindness (= kindly)
by accident (= accidentally)
by luck (= luckily)
on purpose (= purposedly)

제11강 명사와 관사

> He did it **with ease**.
> We treated her **with kindness**.
> **By** good **luck**, I found him at home.
> He broke my glasses **on purpose**.

3) have the + 추상명사 + to 부정사 ~하게도 …하다

> He **had the kindness to show** me the way
> = He **was so kind as to show** me the way.
> = He **was kind enough to show** me the way.
> = He **kindly showed** me the way.

4) to one's 감정의 추상명사 ~하게도

> **To his disappointment**, she was not there.
> **To my surprise**, he won the first prize in the contest.

5) 추상명사 + itself = all + 추상명사 = very + 형용사

> He is **kindness itself**.
> = He is **all kindness**.
> = He is **very kind**.

5. 집합명사의 수

1) 일정 구성원을 가진 집합체

family, committee, audience, team, class, jury 등
집단 자체를 가리키면 단수 취급하며, 집단의 구성원을 가리키면 복수 취급한다.

> His **family** *is* very large. **It** *is* a large family. **It** *consists* of 9 members.
> His **family** *are* all very kind. **They** always *help* the poor.

2) 불특정 수의 무리: 항상 복수 취급

people, cattle, poultry, vermin 등

> **People** *say* that he is guilty.
> **Cattle** *are* grazing on the grass.

(cf.) many **people** 많은 사람들
　　 many **peoples** 많은 민족들

3) 특정 사회계층 전체: 보통 정관사 the가 붙고, 항상 복수 취급

　 the police, the clergy, the nobility, the aristocracy, the public 등

> **The police** *are* searching for a tall dark man with a beard.

6. 명사의 수량 표시

1) many + 복수 가산명사
　much + 단수 불가산명사

> He has **many friends** in Japan.
> He has **much money** in his account.

2) a great[good] many + 복수명사

> **A great many students** have seen the sight.
> I spent **a good many years** working in the Middle East.

3) many a + 단수명사 (+ 단수동사)

> **Many a student** *likes* music.
> **Many a little** *makes* a mickle.

4) a (great/ good) number of + 복수명사 (+ 복수동사)

> **A good number of tenants** *have* been evicted for not paying the rent.
> **A number of students** *were* present at the meeting.

(cf.) the number of + 복수명사 (+ 단수동사)
　　 The number of students at the meeting *was* very small.

5) a great[good] deal of
   = a(n) (large/ great) amount of + 단수명사 (+ 단수동사)

   > This book requires **a great deal of concentration**.

6) a lot of, lots of, plenty of = many, much <가산명사, 불가산명사 모두 가능>

   > This fish has **a lot of bones** in it.
   > I've got **a lot of homework** tonight.

7) few + 복수 가산명사 <부정의 개념>
   a few + 복수 가산명사 <긍정의 개념>
   little + 불가산명사 <부정의 개념>
   a little + 불가산명사 <긍정의 개념>

   > There are **few apples**.
   > There are **a few apples**.
   > I have **little money**.
   > I have **a little money**.

   (cf.) quite a few[little] = not a few[little] 적지 않은, 꽤 많은
   only a few[little] = very few[little] 극히 적은, 거의 없는
   I have **quite a few friends**.
   I have **only a little money**.

7. 불가산명사의 수량 표시

1) 물질명사

   '단위명사 + of + 물질명사'로 나타낸다. 둘 이상을 나타낼 때에는 물질명사를 복수로 만들지 않고, 단위명사를 복수로 한다.

   > **a sheet of** paper, **two sheets of** paper
   > **a glass of** water, **two glasses of** water
   > **a slice of** toast, **two slices of** toast
   > **a pound of** sugar, **two pounds of** sugar
   > **a loaf of** bread, **two loaves of** bread

2) 집합적 물질명사

관사 없이 쓰고 항상 단수로 취급하며, much, little, a little 등으로 수식이 가능하지만, many, few, a few로는 수식이 불가능하다.

```
There was *an equipment in the office. (×)
There was little equipment in the office. (○)
There *were *many furnitures in the office. (×)
There was much furniture in the office. (○)
```

3) 추상명사

'단위명사+of+추상명사'로 나타낸다. 둘 이상을 나타낼 때에는 추상명사를 복수로 만들지 않고, 단위명사를 복수로 한다.

```
many pieces of advice
a case of theft
some bits of information
a stroke of luck
a fit of fever
```

8. 불규칙 복수형

1) 외래어 복수

① -on → -a

```
phenomenon → phenomena          criterion → criteria
```

② -sis → -ses

```
basis → bases      thesis → theses      hypothesis → hypotheses
crisis → crises    analysis → analyses  oasis → oases
```

③ -us → -i

```
focus → foci       stimulus → stimuli   alumnus → alumni
```

④ -a → -ae

formula → formulae   antenna → antennae   larva → larvae

⑤ -um → -a

dat**um** → dat**a**   medi**um** → medi**a**

2) 복합명사의 복수형

father**s**-in-law, looker**s**-on, passer**s**-by, **women**-writers, **men**-servants, merry-go-round**s**, have-not**s**, tooth-brush**es**, tooth-pick**s**, man-eater**s** 등

3) 단수와 복수의 형태가 같은 명사

deer, sheep, swine, fish, salmon, carp, trout, Chinese, Japanese, Vietnamese, Swiss, series, species, means, aircraft, spacecraft 등

9. 유의해야 할 복수명사의 용법

1) 복수형이라도 단수로 취급하는 명사

학문명: mathematics, economics, ethics, physics, politics, statistics 등
질병명: measles, diabetes, rickets 등
게임명: billiards, checkers 등
국명/기타: the United States, the United Nations, the Philippines, news 등

Mathematics *is* both an art and a science.
The United States *consists* of 50 states.
Bad **news** *travels* quickly.

(cf.) statistics가 '통계(수치)'의 의미로 쓰였을 때는 복수로 취급한다.
   Statistics *is* a branch of mathematics. 〈통계학〉
   Statistics *show* that the population of the country is 1 billion. 〈통계〉

2) 상호복수

2개 이상의 단어가 상호적으로 작용하여 하나의 동작을 이루는 경우에는 명사를 복수형으로 써야 한다.

> shake **hands** with(악수하다), change **trains[cars]**(열차를 갈아타다), change **seats** with(~와 자리를 바꾸다), make **friends** with(~와 친해지다), take **turns** (교대하다), be on good **terms** with(~와 사이가 좋다) 등

3) 짝으로 이루어진 사물의 이름

compasses, glasses, gloves, pants, scissors, shoes 등
복수로 취급하고, a pair of를 사용하여 개수를 센다.

> His **trousers** *were* covered in mud.
> *A pair of* **glasses** gave her an urban intelligent look.
> He should not have bought *three pairs of* **shoes**.

4) 분화복수

복수가 되면 의미가 달라지는 명사를 의미한다.

advices 통지	airs 건방진 태도	arms 무기
authorities 당국	brains 학력	colors 깃발
contents 목차	customs 세관	glasses 안경
goods 상품	manners 예절	numbers 시가(詩歌)
pains 수고	parts 재능	provisions 양식
quarters 숙소	regards 안부	waters 해양
sands 사막	works 공장	letters 학식
means 수단; 재산	savings 저축	damages 손해배상금
spectacles 안경	dues 회비	futures 선물(先物)
facilities 시설		

> **Arms** are weapons, especially bombs and guns.
> He is a man of **means**.
> Total **damages** were estimated at $490,000.

10. 수량명사

hundred, thousand, million, billion, dozen(12), score(20) 등

1) 일정한 수사 뒤에 오면 -s 없는 복수형

> **two dozen** eggs (24개의)
> **three score** books (60권의)
> **five hundred** attendants
> **several million** inhabitants
> Five ***hundreds** of students were present. (×)
> Five **hundred** students were present. (○)
> = Five **hundred** of the students were present.

2) 막연한 수량을 나타내면 -s 복수형 + of

> **dozens of** eggs (수십 개의)
> **scores of** books (수십 권의)
> **hundreds of** people (수백 명의)
> **millions of** inhabitants (수백만 명의)

11. 종류·유형 명사

1) a kind[sort/ type] of + 무관사 단수명사 (+ 단수동사)
kinds[sorts/ types] of + 무관사 복수명사 (+ 복수동사)

> **a kind[sort/ type] of** *book*
> **kinds[sorts/ types] of** *books*
> **This kind of** *flower is* rare in Korea.
> **These kinds of** *flowers are* rare in Korea.

(cf.) of 뒤에서는 단수형 종류표시 명사로 복수형 명사를 수식할 수 있다.
  flowers of **this kind** (○)

2) 불가산명사는 종류 표시어가 복수형이라 해도 단수로 쓴다.

> *these kinds of* ***furnitures** (×)
> *these kinds of* **furniture** (○)

12. 수사 + 명사

수사가 명사와 하이픈으로 연결되어 일종의 형용사와 같은 역할을 하는 경우, 명사는 단수형으로 쓴다.

a **ten-dollar** bill
a **five-story** building
a **three-hour** class
a **twelve-year-old** boy
the **five-mile-long** river
She has a **three-*years-old** daughter. (×)
She has a **three-year-old** daughter. (○)
He is a **six-*feet-tall** man. (×)
He is a **six-foot-tall** man. (○)

(cf.) She is three years old.
　　　He is six feet tall.

13. 명사 + 명사

'명사 + 명사' 구조의 복합명사에서는 앞의 명사가 뒤의 명사를 설명하는 역할을 하며, 앞의 명사는 단수형이 원칙이다. 복수인 경우에는 뒤의 명사를 복수형으로 쓴다.

a bus driver 버스 운전기사
brain operation 뇌수술
body weight 몸무게
intelligence test 지능검사
blood type 혈액형

a book store 서점
a corner table 코너용 탁자
a phone book 전화번호부
a stone bridge 돌다리
tennis shoes 테니스화

(cf.) 복수형으로 의미가 유지되는 명사, 학문명 등은 앞의 명사인 경우에도 복수형으로 쓴다.

a **mathematics** teacher
savings account
futures market 선물(先物) 시장

customs officer
nuclear arms control
sales department

14. 이중소유격

소유격이 a, an, this, that, some, any, no, another 등의 다른 한정사와 중복되는 경우, '한정사 + 명사 + of + 소유대명사' 형태의 이중소유격으로 써야 한다.

*my that book (×)	that book of mine (○)
*Tom's a friend (×)	a friend of Tom's (○)
*another her dress (×)	another dress of hers (○)
*her mother's some rings (×)	some rings of her mother's (○)
It's *no your business. (×)	It's no business of yours. (○)

(cf.) This is **my father's car**. 〈아버지 차가 한 대인 경우〉
This is **a car of my father's**. 〈아버지가 소유하고 있는 여러 차 중의 한 대〉
a portrait of my father 〈아버지를 그린 초상화〉
a portrait of my father's 〈아버지가 소유하고 있는 초상화 중의 하나〉

15. 독립소유격

소유격 다음의 명사가 생략되는 경우

1) 명사가 반복되는 경우

This book is **Tom's** (book).
My car is larger than **Tom's** (car).

2) house, shop, store, office, cathedral 등의 알 수 있는 건물 표시 명사의 생략

My father has just been to **the barber's** (shop).
I visited my **teacher's** (house).
Have you ever been to **St. Paul's** (Cathedral)?

16. 무생물에 -'s 소유격을 쓰는 경우

1) 특정시점, 기간, 거리, 금액, 중량 등의 척도

today's weather forecast <특정 시점>
three days' journey <기간>
ten miles' distance <거리>
five dollars' worth of flour <금액>
a pound's weight <중량>

2) 관용구

within[at] a **stone's** throw 엎어지면 코 닿을 데
by a **hair's** breadth 간발의 차이로, 아슬아슬하게
at one's **wit's[wits]'** end 어찌할 바를 모르고
at one's **fingers'** ends ~에 정통한
for **heaven's sake** 제발
for **convenience('s)** sake 편의상

My school is **within a stone's throw** from the bus stop.
I was **at my wit's end** because of her sudden appearance.

17. 부정관사의 용법

1) 많은 사물 중 불특정의 어느 하나를 가리키면 명사 앞에 a(n)를 붙인다.

Tom is **a** kind boy.
on **a** rainy night

(cf.) 특성 대상으로 한정되는 경우는 정관사
   on the morning of May 5
(cf.) 한정되는 명사일지라도 많은 사물 중의 어느 하나이면 a가 붙을 수 있다.
   a teacher of my school
   a dress of that color

2) 철자가 아니라 발음을 기준으로 자음 앞에는 a, 모음 앞에는 an을 쓴다.

> **a** useful thing <[j]는 자음으로 취급>
> **a** one-eyed Jack <[w]는 자음으로 취급>
> **a** Europe
> **an** M.P.
> **an** honest man <h가 묵음인 경우>
> **an** heir <h가 묵음인 경우>

3) 부정관사의 의미

① **one** 하나의

Rome was not built in **a** day.

② **the same** 동일한

Birds of **a** feather flock together.

③ **every, per** 매 ~마다 / ~당

We'll drive at 60 miles **an** hour.

④ **a certain** 어떤

In **a** sense he is a victim.
A Mr. Smith came to see you in your absence.

⑤ **some** 약간의

The detective followed him at **a** distance.
We stayed there for **a** while.

⑥ **any** 종족대표, 대표단수

A dog is a faithful animal.

18. 정관사의 용법

1) 앞에 나온 명사가 다시 나올 때

I have a dog. **The** dog is white.

2) 이미 알고 있거나 전후 관계로 알 수 있는 것을 말할 때

Open **the** door, please.
The post office is near **the** station.
Sam, you are wanted on **the** phone.

3) 유일한 사물, 직책, 사건 및 방위

the sun, **the** moon, **the** earth, **the** sea, **the** sky, **the** universe, **the** galaxy, **the** world, **the** president, **the** Korean War, **the** east[west/ south/ north], **the** right[left] 등

(cf.) 태양, 달, 지구 이외의 천체명은 무관사이다.
　*the Venus (×) → Venus (○)
　*the Mars (×) → Mars (○)

4) 수식어구로 한정될 때

The water *of this well* is not good to drink.
He has **the** wisdom *of Solomon*.
London is **the** capital *of England*.

(cf.) 특정되지 않고 여러 사람 중의 한 사람임을 의미할 때
　He is **a** teacher *of our school.*
　He is **an** old man *who lives in our neighborhood.*

5) 서수, 최상급, only, same, last 등이 붙는 명사 앞에

I took **the first** train.
Jane is **the tallest** girl in our class.
You are **the only** man for the job.
They met in **the same** place as before.
He is **the last** man to tell a lie.

6) 종족의 대표를 나타낼 때

The dog is a faithful animal.
= A dog is a faithful animal.
= Dogs are faithful animals.

7) 전치사 by와 함께 시간, 수량의 단위를 나타낼 때

Sugar is sold **by the pound**. <파운드 당>
Most of the rooms in that hotel are paid **by the hour**. <시간 당>

8) 신체의 일부 표시

① 잡다, 쥐다(catch, hold, take, seize 등) → by

He *caught* me **by the hand**.
He *caught* me by *my hand. (×)

② 접촉(touch, pat, hit, kiss, strike 등) → on

He *struck* me **on the head**.
He *struck* me on *my head. (×)

③ 보다(look, stare, gaze 등) → in

He *looked* me **in the face**.
He *looked* me in *my face. (×)

19. the + 형용사/분사

1) 복수보통명사 (~한 사람들)

The rich *are* not always happy. (= rich people)
The idle *are* apt to get up late morning.
The unemployed *want* their jobs back.
The dying and **the wounded** *were* carried from the battlefield.

2) 추상명사

The beautiful *is* higher than **the true**.
= **Beauty** is higher than **truth**.

3) 단수보통명사

the deceased(고인(故人)), the accused(피고) 등

The deceased *was* identified as Thomas.
The accused *was* sentenced to life imprisonment.

20. 유의해야 할 관사의 위치

1) quite/ rather/ such/ what + a(n) + 형용사 + 명사

Teaching is **quite a good job**.
He is **rather a nervous man**.
We had **such a good time**.
What a good job it is! <감탄문>

2) so/ as/ too/ how + 형용사 + a(n) + 명사

I've never seen **so clever an animal**. (= such a clever animal)
Teaching is **too good a job** to give up.
How big a building it is! <감탄문>

3) all/ both/ double/ half/ twice + the + 명사

All the boys are pleased with their Christmas presents.
I paid **twice[double/ half] the price** for the same pen.

21. 관사의 생략

1) 장소, 건물 명사가 본래의 목적으로 쓰일 때

go to school 수업하러 가다
go to church 예배드리러 가다
go to sea 선원이 되다
go to bed 잠자리에 들다

> The bakers go to **church** every Sunday. <본래 목적>
> He goes to **the church** to meet his girlfriend every Sunday. <다른 목적>

2) 유일 직책, 혈연관계 등이 동격이나 보어로 쓰일 경우

> George Bush, **President of the USA**, was present at the meeting. <동격>
> They elected George as **chairman**. <보어>
> John, **son of a minister**, visited my house. <동격, 혈연관계>

3) 관직[신분] 뒤에 인명이 오는 경우

> **President** Donald Trump will meet Chinese Vice Premier Liu He at the White House.

4) by 뒤의 교통[통신]수단은 무관사가 원칙이다.

> I usually go to work **by subway**.
> I'll inform you **by phone**.
> I'll watch the game **on TV**.

(cf.) by 이외의 전치사의 경우에는 관사가 온다.
  in a car, on a bike, over the telephone 등

5) 식사, 운동, 병명, 학과

> have **breakfast**, have **lunch**, have **dinner**, play **tennis**, play **baseball**, play **soccer**, get **cancer**, die of **cancer**, died of **measles**, major in **economics** **[physics/ mathematics]** 등

(cf.) 특정한 식사, 형용사가 앞에 오는 경우 부정관사가 온다.
  a heavy dinner, a very nice lunch

(cf.) 'have + 병명'의 경우 부정관사가 온다.
    have a headache, have a cold
(cf.) 악기 앞에는 정관사가 온다.
    play **the violin**
    play **the piano**

6) 대구를 이루는 표현

> day and night, hand in hand, face to face, side by side, step by step, from door to door, live from hand to mouth 등

22. 고유명사와 정관사

1) 정관사가 붙는 경우

바다 the Pacific Ocean	강 the Mississippi
해협 the Straits of Korea	반도 the Korean Peninsula
사막 the Sahara	산맥 the Himalayas
신문 the Times	호텔 the Grand Hotel
국민 the French, the Chinese	관공서 the White House, the Pentagon
선박 the Mayflower, 열차, 항공기 등	

2) 관사가 붙지 않는 경우

호수 Lake Michigan	산 Mt. Everest
섬 Jejudo	도시 New York, Paris
대학 Oxford University	공원 Central Park
거리 Main Street, Fifth Avenue	언어 French, Chinese
지명을 동반하는 공공건물 Seoul Station, Incheon International Airport 등	

대명사(Pronoun)

1. 인칭대명사의 격과 수일치

1) 주어와 주격 보어 자리에는 주격 대명사를 쓰고, 목적어와 목적격 보어 자리에는 목적격 대명사를 쓰는 것이 원칙이다.

> I love **her** and **she** loves **me**, too.
> The man who broke the window was ***him**, not ***me**. (×)
> The man who broke the window was **he**, not **I**. (○)
> She thought the man to be ***I**. (×)
> She thought the man to be **me**. (○)

2) 전치사의 뒤에는 목적격을 쓴다.

> Let's keep it secret *between* **you** and **me**.
> She kissed everyone *but* **me**.

3) 소유격 뒤의 명사가 생략되면 소유대명사를 쓴다.

> She has a car. This car is **hers**. (= her car)

4) 이중소유격 표현에서 of 뒤에는 소유대명사가 온다.

> It's no business of *****you**. (×)
> It's no business of **yours**. (○)

5) 비교 대상은 동일한 격을 쓰는 것이 원칙이다.

> **She** likes you better than **I**. <She와 I가 비교대상>
> She likes **you** better than **me**. <you와 me가 비교대상>

6) 인칭대명사는 선행하는 명사와 수가 일치해야 한다.

> In a pre-industrial society most *people* spent **their** lives in **their** own village.

2. 인칭대명사 it의 용법

1) 앞에서 언급한 특정의 사물이나 구, 절, 문장 등을 가리킬 경우

> He took a stone and threw **it**. (it = the stone)
> The prisoner attempted to escape, but found **it** impossible.
> (it = to escape)
> You saved my life; I'll never forget **it**. (it = that you saved my life)

2) 신원이 확인되지 않은 사람

> *Someone* was moving stealthily in the darkness; **it** was a burglar.

3) 비인칭주어

> **It**'s fine today. <날씨>
> **It**'s Sunday today. <시간>
> How far is **it** from here to the airport? <거리>
> How much is **it**? <금액>
> How is **it** going? <상황>

4) 가주어, 가목적어

> **It** is certain *that Mary will go with me*.
> She made **it** clear *that she didn't want to contact you*.

5) 강조 구문의 주어

*He was my son that won the first prize. (×)
It was my son that won the first prize. (○)
*They were only 3 people that were injured in the accident. (×)
It was only 3 people that were injured in the accident. (○)

3. 재귀대명사

1) 재귀적 용법

① 행위의 주체와 대상이 일치하는 경우, 목적어는 재귀대명사를 써야 한다.

He killed **him**. <살인, He ≠ him>
He killed **himself**. <자살, He = himself>
Heaven helps those who help **themselves**.

② 재귀대명사는 반드시 동일절 내에 지시대상이 있어야 하며, 종속절의 재귀대명사가 주절의 주어를 가리킬 수는 없다.

I did not think that you could hurt ***myself*** this way. (×)
I did not think that you could hurt **me** this way. (○)
He said that Mary didn't like ***himself***. (×)
He said that Mary didn't like **him**. (○)

2) 강조적 용법

주어, 목적어, 명사 등을 강조하는 부사적 역할을 한다. '몸소', '직접', '그 자체로서'라는 의미를 가진다.

She did it **herself**.
= She **herself** did it.
Life **itself** is an unsolved mystery. <주어 강조>
I can't believe you saw the man **himself**. <타동사의 목적어 강조>
What you are searching for is in you **yourself**. <전치사의 목적어 강조>

3) 재귀대명사의 관용표현: 전치사 + 재귀대명사

> by oneself 혼자서
> of itself 저절로
> beside oneself 제정신이 아닌, 이성을 잃은
> in spite of oneself 자신도 모르게
> between ourselves 우리끼리 얘긴데
>
> for oneself 혼자 힘으로
> in itself 그 자체로, 본래

The problem is trivial **in itself**.
They were **beside themselves** with joy.
I said so **in spite of myself**.

4) 재귀동사

관용적으로 재귀대명사를 목적어로 하는 동사들이 있다.

> absent oneself from 결석하다
> addict oneself to ~에 빠지다, 탐닉하다
> apply oneself to 전념하다
> avail oneself of ~을 이용하다
> devote oneself to 전념하다, 헌신하다
> enjoy oneself 즐겁게 지내다
> exert oneself to 노력하다
> seat oneself 앉다
> help oneself to ~을 마음껏 많이 드세요
> immerse oneself in ~에 열중하다
> lose oneself 길을 잃다
> make oneself at home 편안히 하다
> oversleep oneself 늦잠자다

4. this/ that

1) 앞 명사의 반복을 피하는 that, those

반복되는 명사 뒤에 수식어구가 있는 경우에 쓴다.

> The climate of Korea is milder than **that** *of England*. <that = the climate>
> The apples in this box are not so big as **those** *in that box*.
> <those = the apples>

2) those who ~한 사람들

> **Those who** like borrowing dislike paying.
> Blessed are **those who** mourn, for they will be comforted.

(cf.) 관계대명사의 선행사로 they, them은 올 수 없다.
   I like *****them who** are honest. (×)
   I like **those who** are honest. (○)

(cf.) one who ~하는 사람
   I'm the **one who** should receive an apology.

3) that = 전자 / this = 후자

> Jason loves Miranda; **that** is 26 and **this** is three years younger.

4) this, that의 부사적 용법

정도나 양을 나타내는 형용사나 부사를 수식하여 '그처럼', '그만큼'의 뜻으로 사용된다.

> I've never been out **this** *late* before. <= to this degree>
> She returned home **that** *late*. <= so>

5. such

1) such as ~와 같은

> **such** subjects **as** English and math
> = subjects **such as** English and math
> = subjects **like** English and math

(cf.) **such** subjects ***like** English and math (×)

2) as such 그렇게, 그 자체로서(= in itself)

I am a foreigner and want to be treated **as such**.
Technology, **as such**, is neither good nor bad.

(cf.) such가 be동사의 보어일 경우에는 흔히 도치가 일어난다.
My reward *was* **such**.
= **Such** *was my reward*.
His anxiety *was* **such** that he lost his health.
= **Such** *was his anxiety* that he lost his health.

6. so

1) that절 수반 동사 뒤에서 앞 절의 내용을 다시 언급하고자 할 때 쓴다.
think, believe, suppose, hope, expect, be afraid 등

Do you think[hope/ believe/ expect] that she will come to the party?
— I think **so**. (= I think that she will come to the party.)
— I'm afraid **so**. (= I'm afraid that she will come to the party.)

(cf.) 부정문의 경우
 think, believe, suppose 등의 think류 동사 뒤
 I **don't** think[believe/ suppose] **so**. (= I think **not**.)
 hope, expect, say, be afraid 등의 동사 뒤
 I hope[am afraid] **not**.
 I *****don't** hope **so**. (×)

2) be, become, keep, remain 등이 쓰인 2형식 문장에서 앞의 명사, 형용사를 대신함

If airplanes are dangerous, cars are much more **so**. <so = dangerous>
He became president in 1980, and remained **so** for 7 years.
<so = president>

7. one

1) 일반인

One should keep **one's[his]** promise, or at least try to keep it.

2) 앞에 나온 'a + 단수 가산명사'를 받는다.

If you need a book, I will lend you **one**. <one = a book>

(cf.) 'the + 명사'는 it으로 받는다.
I bought the pen last week, but somebody took **it**. ⟨it = the pen⟩

3) 형용사의 수식을 받는 경우에는 부정관사를 붙이고, 복수형은 수식어를 동반한다.

I don't like this hat. Can you show me **a better one**?
Do you have a knife? Yes, I have some **sharp ones**.

(cf.) 수식어구가 한정하는 특정한 명사를 받는 경우에는 the를 붙인다.
The lady is **the** one whom I met last month.

4) one을 사용할 수 없는 경우

① 불가산명사

This *furniture* is different from that ***one**. (×)
I like red *wine* better than white ***one**. (×)

② 소유격, 기수, both, these, those 뒤

My hat is smaller than *Mary's* ***one**. (×)
We need some bowls. I will buy *five* ***ones**. (×)
If you want to read these books, you can take *both/ these/ those* ***ones**. (×)

8. some/ any

1) some은 긍정문에 쓰고, any는 부정문, 의문문, 조건문에 쓴다.

Do you have **any** friends in the United States? <의문문>
— Yes, I have **some** friends in Texas. <긍정문>
— No, I don't have **any** friends who live in America. <부정문>
If you have **any** good idea, please let us know. <조건문>

2) 권유, 부탁, 제의, 요청 등의 긍정적 대답을 기대할 경우에는 의문문, 조건문에도 some을 쓴다.

Would you like **some** more beer?
Do you mind if I play **some** music on?

3) any를 긍정문에 쓰면 '어떤 ~라도 다'의 뜻이다.

Any boy can see the film if he is over 12.

4) 부정문에서 any를 주어에 쓰지 않는다.

*__Anyone didn't die__ in the accident. (×)
No one died in the accident. (○)

9. every/ each

1) each는 형용사와 대명사로 쓰인다.

each + 단수 가산명사 + 단수동사
each of + 한정사 + 복수명사 + 단수동사
each + 단수동사

Each *country has* its own customs. <each = 형용사>
Each of *the girls was* dressed neatly. <each = 대명사>
Each *has* his own car. <each = 대명사>

2) every는 형용사로만 쓰인다.

every + 단수 가산명사

> **Every** *dog* has his day.
> **Every** *man, woman, and child* has been evacuated.

(cf.) *****Every** of the boys has his computer. (×)
　　Each of the boys has his computer. (○)

　　*****Every** knows her. (×)
　　Everybody/ Everyone knows her. (○)

3) every + 기수 + 복수명사 = every + 서수 + 단수명사 매 ~마다

> The olympics are held **every four years**.
> = The olympics are held **every fourth year**.

(cf.) I go to the dentist's **every other day**. (격일로)
　　(= every second day, every two days)

10. all/ most/ almost

1) all은 대명사와 형용사로 쓰인다.

all + 복수 가산명사/불가산명사
all + (of) + 한정사 + 명사

> **All** *things* being equal, we should finish the job tomorrow. <형용사>
> **All** *life* is a series of struggles. <형용사>
> **All** *the cities* in Iraq were destroyed. <전치한정사>
> **All** were happy. <대명사, 모든 사람들>
> **All** that glitters is not gold. <대명사, 모든 것>

(cf.) She was dressed **all** in white. 〈부사〉

2) most는 대명사와 형용사로 쓰인다.

most + 복수 가산명사/불가산명사
most + of + 한정사 + 명사

Most *people* agree with my opinion. <형용사>
I spent **most** *time* on the first question. <형용사>
Most of the *players* on the team earn more money than we. <대명사>

3) almost는 부사이므로 명사를 직접 수식할 수 없으나, all과 같은 부정대명사나 every, all, no, any와 같은 부정형용사는 수식할 수 있다.

***Almost** employees participated in the strike. (×)
Almost all of the employees participated in the strike. (○)
He comes here **almost every** day.

11. other/ another

1) 대상이 둘일 때, 하나는 one, 나머지 하나는 the other로 표현한다.

I have two dogs; **one** is white and **the other** is black.
Let it go in **one** ear and out **the other**.

2) 대상이 셋 이상인 경우

```
하나: one    —    나머지 전부: the others
하나: one    —    또 하나: another
일부: some   —    또 다른 일부: others
일부: some   —    나머지 전부: the others
```

There are six books; **one** is mine, and **the others** are his.
One boy went home, and **another** stayed at school.
Some like fall; **others** like spring.
There are 50 students; **some** study English and **the others** study French.

3) another의 기타 용법

① 하나 더, 또 하나의(= one more)

Please give me **another** cup of tea.

② 다른 것(= a different one)

I don't like this book; show me **another**.

③ 역시, 마찬가지(= also one)

He is a liar, and his wife is **another**.

④ 관용표현
   A is one thing, B is another. A와 B는 별개다.

To know is **one thing**; to teach is **another**.
Making money is **one thing** and spending money is **another**.
= Making money is quite different from spending money.

4) another + 단수 가산명사
   other + 복수명사/불가산명사

If you don't like this tie, I'll show you **another** *tie*.
Please show me **other** *shoes*.

(cf.) another + 수사 + 복수명사
   In **another two years**, the project will be finished with satisfaction.

5) 상호대명사

each other <둘 사이에>
one another <셋 이상에>

Jack and Susie really loved **each other**.
The three countries are trading with **one another** more than ever before.

12. none/ no

1) none은 대명사로만 쓰인다.

None of + 가산 복수명사 + 단수/복수동사
None of + 불가산명사 + 단수동사

None *have* succeeded in solving it.
None of *us want/ wants* to die.
None of *the water is* worth drinking.

2) no + 무관사 가산명사 = not + a/ any + 명사

I have **no** *friend* in Busan.
= I have **not a** *friend* in Busan. <not은 부사>
= I do not have a/ any friend in Busan.

13. either/ neither

대명사와 형용사로 쓰이며 단수 취급한다.
지시대상이 둘일 경우에 쓴다.
either/ neither of + 복수명사
either/ neither + 단수명사

Either of *the two boys is* honest.
Neither of *the two boys was* present.
Either *day is* OK.
Neither *statement is* true.

형용사(Adjective)

1. 한정적 용법

1) 전치 수식

He is suffering from a **serious** illness.
There was not an **empty** seat in the bus.

2) 후치 수식

① 형용사 뒤에 수식어구가 동반될 때

I have a dictionary **useful** for children.

② -thing, -body, -one 을 수식할 때

There was *something* **sharp** in her shoe.
I have *nothing* **particular** to do this afternoon.

③ -able, -ible 로 끝나는 형용사가 all, every, 최상급 다음에 오는 명사를 수식할 때

You have to use *the latest* information **available**.
He has tried *every* means **possible** to find a job.

④ 서술적 형용사가 명사를 수식할 때

> He is the greatest poet **alive**.
> The members **present** were in favor of his suggestion.

⑤ 관용어구

> from time **immemorial** 태곳적부터
> president **elect** 대통령 당선자
> the authorities **concerned** 관계당국
>
> Asia **Minor** 소아시아
> the sum **total** 총계
> a poet **laureate** 계관시인

⑥ 한정적 용법으로만 쓰는 형용사
drunken, elder, former, golden, inner, latter, lone, mere, sheer, sole, thorough, upper, utmost, utter, wooden 등

> His **elder** brother lives in New York.
> He is an **utter** stranger to me.
> That **wooden** floor creaks when we walk on it.

2. 서술적 용법

1) 주격 보어나 목적격 보어로 쓰일 때

> His excuse sounds **strange**, but it is true. <주격 보어>
> The neighbour found him **dead** on his bed. <목적격 보어>

(cf.) 준보어
> He returned **alive**.
> My father married **young**.

2) 서술적 용법으로만 쓰는 형용사

① a-로 시작되는 형용사
afraid, alike, alive, alone, ashamed, asleep, awake, aware 등

> She is **afraid** of going there on her own.
> We remain confident that he is still **alive**.
> She was **awake** every night because of insomnia.

(cf.) All **living** things need water to live.

② 감정을 나타내는 형용사 및 기타
content, fond, glad, liable, unable, upset, worth 등

> They are **content** with their present salary.
> He is **fond** of finding fault with others.
> All men are **liable** to envy other people's happiness.

3. 한정적 용법과 서술적 용법에 따라 의미가 다른 형용사

1) certain 어떤 / 확실한

> He arrived at a **certain** town.
> It is **certain** that they will agree.

2) ill 나쁜 / 아픈

> **Ill** news runs apace.
> He cannot go with you because he is **ill** in bed.

3) late 고(故) / 늦은

> The **late** Mr. Brown was a very sincere politician.
> He had overslept and was **late** for his job interview.

4) present 현재의 / 출석한

> The policy of the **present** Cabinet is not appropriate.
> We were all **present** at the graduation ceremony.

5) right 오른쪽의(한정) / 옳은(한정, 서술)

> One woman has a microphone in her **right** hand.
> Sometimes, the **right** question is more important than the **right** answer.
> It was quite **right** of you to refuse the offer.

4. 전치사적 형용사

전치사처럼 바로 뒤에 목적어를 취한다.
like, unlike, near, worth, opposite 등

> She was **like** her mother in many respects.
> A woman was standing **near** the door.
> This book is **worth** reading.

1) like vs. alike

> His brother looks just **like** him. <전치사적 형용사>
> He and his brother look **alike**. <서술형용사>

2) worth vs. worthy

> The picture is **worth** *of two thousand pounds. (×)
> The picture is **worth** two thousand pounds. (○)
> The book is **worth** *to read twice. (×)
> The book is **worth reading** twice. (○)
> = The book is **worthy to be read** twice.

5. 형용사의 열거 순서

1) 명사 수식어의 순서
전치한정사 + 한정사 + 수사(서수 + 기수) + 일반형용사 + 파생형용사 + 명사

> **the first three** months in the year
> **the world's three largest** cities
> for **half an** hour <half는 전치한정사>
> **a new world** record <world는 형용사 역할>
> **the first three beautiful Italian leather** handbags

(cf.) 전치한정사

all, both, half, 배수사(double, twice, three times) 등으로, all, both, half 뒤에는 전치사 of가 올 수 있지만, 배수사 뒤에는 전치사 of가 올 수 없다.

all (of) the soldiers
both (of) his brothers
half (of) the water
all/ both/ half of *them* 〈대명사가 올 때는 반드시 전치사 of가 쓰임〉
double *of the speed (×)
double the speed (○)

2) 일반형용사의 어순

대소 + 형상 + 성질 + 신구 + 재료

a **large round new wooden** table

6. 수사 표현

1) 명사 + 수사

① 순서가 있는 경우
  the + 서수 + 명사 = 명사 + 기수

```
act Ⅰ = the first act = act one
chapter Ⅴ = the fifth chapter = chapter five
lesson 10 = the tenth lesson = lesson ten
volume Ⅲ = the third volume = volume three
World War Ⅱ = the Second World War = World War Two
```

(cf.) 인명 + 숫자 (서수로 읽음)
  Napoleon Ⅲ = Napoleon **the Third**
  Elizabeth Ⅱ = Elizabeth **the Second**

② 순서가 없는 경우
  명사 + 기수

```
Flight 14 = Flight fourteen
Gate 4 = Gate four
Room 2 = Room two
```

2) 분수

분자는 기수, 분모는 서수로 읽는다. 분자가 2 이상일 때 분모는 복수로 한다.

```
1/2 = a[one] half          1/3 = a[one] third
1/4 = a[one] quarter       2/3 = two-thirds
3/4 = three-fourths
```

3) 척도표시 형용사

척도표시 형용사는 척도명사 다음에 온다.

```
That building has a wall ten feet thick.
The tower is five hundred feet high.
= The tower is five hundred feet in height.
```

7. 가주어-진주어 구문

1) It is + 형용사 + for + O + to부정사

hard, difficult, easy, tough, possible, impossible, dangerous, nice, good, pleasant 등
부정사의 목적어를 문장의 주어로 쓸 수 있다.

It is *difficult* **for** me **to persuade** her.
= **She** is *difficult* for me to persuade.

(cf.) It's difficult *that I persuade her. (×)

2) It is + 형용사 + of + O + to부정사

kind, wise, clever, silly, foolish, cruel, brave, careless, rude, wrong, right 등 사람의 성품을 나타내는 형용사가 해당되며, 부정사의 의미상의 주어를 문장의 주어로 쓸 수 있다.

It was very *brave* **of** you **to tell** him the truth.
= **You** were very *brave* to tell him the truth.

3) It is + 형용사 + that S + V

apparent, certain, clear, evident, fortunate, likely, obvious, probable, true, uncertain 등

It was *apparent* **that** she was happy.
It is *likely* **that** these animals were killed last night.

(cf.) certain, uncertain, likely, unlikely의 경우는 사람을 주어로 할 수 있다.
He is *certain* to form such a view of the life of men.
He is *likely* to gather information about political challenges.

4) It is + 형용사 + for + O + to V
= It is + 형용사 + that S + (should) + 동사원형

embarrassing, essential, important, natural, necessary, regrettable, strange, surprising, urgent, vital, wonderful 등
감정적, 이성적 판단의 형용사가 해당된다.

It is *necessary* **for** you **to answer** the question.
= **It** is *necessary* **that** you **(should) answer** the question.

8. 용법에 유의해야 할 형용사

1) high나 low를 수식어나 보어로 하는 명사

cost, demand, income, price, rate, salary, speed, temperature, wage 등

The *price* of this book is **high**.
Many employees complained about **low** salaries.

2) large나 small을 수식어나 보어로 하는 명사

amount, attendance, audience, family, number, population, sum 등

The *number* of applicants was **large**.
There was a **small** *attendance* at the meeting.

9. 혼동하기 쉬운 형용사

1) amiable 상냥한, 호감을 주는
   amicable 우호적인

2) beneficial 유익한(= advantageous, useful)
   beneficent 인정 많은(= benevolent)

3) classic 일류의, 전형적인
   classical 고전주의의, 고전적인

4) comparable 비교할 수 있는, 필적하는
   comparative 비교의, 비교적인(= relative)

5) considerable 상당한; 중요한(= substantial; important)
   considerate 사려 깊은, 이해심 많은(= thoughtful)

6) credible 믿을 만한(= believable)
   credulous 잘 믿는, 속기 쉬운(= gullible)

7) desirable 바람직한
   desirous 원하는

8) economic 경제의, 경제학의
   economical 경제적인, 절약하는(= frugal, thrifty)

9) enviable 부러워할 만한
   envious 부러워하는

10) healthy (신체적으로) 건강한
    healthful 건강에 좋은

11) historic 역사적인, 역사적으로 유명한
    historical 역사적인, 역사에 관한

12) imaginable 상상할 수 있는
    imaginative 상상력이 풍부한
    imaginary 상상[가상]의

13) industrial 산업[공업]의
    industrious 근면한(= assiduous, diligent)

14) ingenuous 솔직한, 순진한(= innocent)
    ingenious 영리한(= clever), 독창적인

15) intelligent 지적인, 총명한
    intellectual 지적인, 지능의
    intelligible 이해할 수 있는, 알기 쉬운(= comprehensible)

16) literal 문자의, 글자 그대로의
    literary 문학의, 문학적인
    literate 읽고 쓸 줄 아는

17) momentary 순간적인(= temporary)
    momentous 중대한, 중요한(= important)

18) respectable 존경할 만한, 훌륭한(= honorable)
    respectful 공손한, 예의 바른(= polite)
    respective 각각의, 각자의(= individual)

19) **sensible** 분별 있는, 현명한(= reasonable, wise)
    sensitive 민감한(= susceptible)
    sensual 관능적인
    sensuous 감각적인
    sensational 선풍적인, 선정적인

20) **successful** 성공적인
    successive 연속적인(= consecutive)

21) **childish** 유치한
    childlike 어린이 같은, 귀여운

22) **contemptible** 경멸받을 만한
    contemptuous 경멸하는, 멸시하는

23) **continuous** (중단 없이) 계속되는
    continual (띄엄띄엄) 계속 (되풀이) 되는

24) **confident** 확신하는, 자신 있는(= certain)
    confidential 은밀한, 비밀의(= secret)

25) **imperative** 꼭 필요한, 단호한
    imperious 고압적인, 오만한; 긴급한, 중요한

26) **luxurious** 호화스러운
    luxuriant 기름진; 풍부한

27) **memorable** 기억될 만한, 잊을 수 없는
    memorial 기념의, 추모의

28) negligent 태만한, 부주의한
    negligible 하찮은, 무시해도 좋은

29) uninterested 무관심한, 냉담한
    disinterested 공평한, 사심이 없는

30) valueless 무가치한, 하찮은
    invaluable 매우 귀중한

부사(Adverb)

1. 부사의 역할

동사, 형용사, 부사, 문장 전체를 수식하는 역할을 한다.

> The doctor *examined* his patient **carefully**. <동사 수식>
> That investment is **too** *risky* for us. <형용사 수식>
> She pronounced the word **very** *slowly*. <부사 수식>
> The pilot avoided a collision by changing course **just** *in time*.
> <부사구 수식>
> My wife wants divorce **simply** *because she is not happy with me*.
> <부사절 수식>
> **Fortunately**, *no one was hurt in the accident*. <문장 전체 수식>

(cf.) **Even** *a child* can know who did right and wrong. 〈명사 수식〉

2. 부사의 형태

1) 일반적으로 형용사에 -ly가 붙으면 부사가 된다.

> easy - easily
> possible - possibly
> simple - simply
> true - truly
> usual - usually

(cf.) 명사 + ly = 형용사
 friendly, costly, lovely, lively, orderly 등

(cf.) 부사로 혼동되는 형용사
 lonely, likely, ugly, silly, cowardly 등

2) -ly가 붙지 않는 부사

형용사와 동일한 형태인 부사

early, enough, near, late, fast, hard, high, ill, right, wrong, far, long 등

3) -ly가 붙으면 의미가 달라지는 부사

① late 늦게
   lately 최근에(= recently)

We arrived an hour **late**.
I think you have spent too much money **lately**.

② hard 열심히; 세게
   hardly 거의 ~않다

The athletes have been practicing very **hard** for the competition.
I could **hardly** endure the pain.

③ high 높게 (위치); 비싸게 (가격)
   highly 대단히 (정도)

He threw the ball **high** into the air.
She is a **highly** educated woman.

④ deep 깊게
   deeply 대단히 (정도)

Still waters run **deep**.
He was **deeply** moved by her speech.

⑤ wide 크게, 활짝
   widely 널리; 상당히 (정도)

The door is **wide** open.
He has travelled **widely**.

⑥ **most** 가장 (최상급); 매우(= very)
　mostly 대개는, 대체로(= mainly)

She's one of the **most** experienced teachers in the district.
You are a **most** unusual person. <most = very>
The tourists in Rome were **mostly** Asians.

3. 부사의 위치

1) 동사를 수식하는 경우

① 자동사를 수식할 때는 동사 뒤에 위치한다.

The rumor *spread* **quickly** throughout the city.

② 타동사를 수식할 때는 동사 앞이나 목적어 뒤에 위치한다.

He *explained* the situation **clearly**.
= He **clearly** *explained* the situation.

(cf.) 타동사 + 부사 + 목적어 (목적어가 길 경우)
　　He understood **perfectly** what his wife felt.

③ 조동사 + 부사 + 본동사
　be동사 + 부사 + ~ing/p.p.

He *could* **scarcely** *recognize* his old friend.
She *is* **rarely** *seen* in public nowadays.

2) 빈도부사와 정도부사는 일반동사 앞, be동사 뒤, 조동사 뒤에 위치한다.

빈도부사: always, often, usually, sometimes, hardly, rarely, never 등
정도부사: almost, barely, fairly, nearly, quite, rather, somewhat 등

He **sometimes** *visits* his aunt.
He *is* **often** late for school.
You *should* **always** obey your parents.

3) still의 위치

① still + 일반동사

> She **still** *dislikes* him.

② be동사[조동사] + still

> He *is* **still** standing.

(cf.) He is standing **still**. (형용사, 유사보어)

③ 부정문에서 조동사 앞에 쓰인다.

> He **still** *hasn't* finished the work.
> = He *hasn't* finished the book **yet**.

4) enough의 위치

수식하는 형용사나 부사 바로 뒤에 위치하며, 보통 'to부정사'나 'for + 명사'를 수반한다.

> I was *foolish* **enough** to believe her.
> She sings *well* **enough**.

(cf.) 형용사 enough는 명사 앞, 뒤 둘 다 가능하다.
> I don't have **enough** *money* to buy a car.
> = I don't have *money* **enough** to buy a car.

4. 문미에 오는 부사의 나열 순서

1) 문미부사는 양태 → 장소 → 빈도 → 시간의 부사 순서로 쓰는 것이 일반적이다.

> She sang [**perfectly**] [**in the town hall**] [**last night**].
> This medicine must be taken [**three times**] [**every day**].

2) 왕래발착동사 뒤에는 장소 → 양태 → 빈도 → 시간의 부사 순서로 쓴다.

> I was taken [to the zoo] [regularly] [as a child].
> He drove [to the hospital] [quickly] [this morning].

3) 같은 종류의 부사구가 여러 개 오면, 작은 단위의 부사를 먼저 쓴다.

> I live **at 225, Yeoksamdong, Gangnamgu, Seoul, Korea**.
> I was born in Seoul, **at about 7 a.m. on Friday, June 25, 1980**.

5. 어법에 유의해야 할 부사

1) very/ much

① very
형용사와 부사의 원급, 현재분사, 형용사화 된 과거분사를 수식한다.

> The food of this restaurant is **very** *delicious*.
> His performance moved the audience **very** *deeply*.
> My father has had a **very** *interesting* life.
> She was **very** *tired* when she arrived home.

② much
형용사와 부사의 비교급 및 최상급, 과거분사, 동사, 형용사구, 부사구를 수식한다.

> The new drugs are **much** *more effective*.
> He is **much** *the tallest* boy in his class.
> He is **much** *interested* in astronomy.
> She doesn't *like* traveling **much**.
> His answer is **much** *to the point*.

(cf.) 긍정문에서 동사를 수식하는 경우에는 very, so, too 등을 수반한다.
   Thank you **very much!**

(cf.) afraid, alike, ashamed, aware 등은 much가 수식하는 것이 원칙이지만, 구어에서는 very도 가능하다.
   He was **much** *ashamed* of his behaviour.

제14강 부사

③ too much + 명사
　much too + 형용사/부사

He is burned out from **too much** *work*.
She is **much too** *old* to have a baby.

2) already/ yet

① **already**: 긍정문 (이미, 벌써)

She has **already** won several medals in the Olympics.
All my friends were **already** there.

(cf.) 의문문에 쓰면 '놀람'의 뜻
　　Is he back **already**?

② **yet**: 부정문 (아직), 의문문 (이미, 벌써)

I have *not* read the book **yet**.
Have you finished your report **yet**?

3) ago/ before

① **ago**는 '시간 + ago'의 형태로 항상 과거시제와 함께 쓰인다.

His father *passed away* **ten years ago**.

② **before**는 '시간 + before'의 형태일 때에는 과거완료와 함께 쓰인다. 단독으로 사용될 때는 '이전에'의 뜻으로, 과거, 현재완료, 과거완료에 모두 쓰인다.

He said that she *had left* home **two years before**.
I *have seen* this picture **before**.

4) too/ either

too는 긍정문에, either는 부정문에 쓴다.

My parents *were* happy with the decision, **too**.
My parents *were not* happy with the decision, **either**.

5) good/ well

good은 형용사로 쓰이고, well은 형용사와 부사로 쓰인다.

She is quite a **good speaker**.
She plays the piano very **well**. <부사>
He is **well** enough to travel. <형용사, 건강한>

6. Two-Word Verb

1) 타동사 + 부사

give up, put on, put off, turn on, turn down, call off, pick up 등

① 목적어가 명사인 경우
   타동사 + 목적어 + 부사
   타동사 + 부사 + 목적어

I can't **give** *the opportunity* **up**.
I can't **give up** *the opportunity*.

② 목적어가 대명사인 경우
   타동사 + 목적어 + 부사

I can't **give** *it* **up**.
I can't **give** *****up** *it*. (×)

2) 자동사 + 전치사

account for, call on, deal with, depend on, look at, look into, wait on 등
자동사 + 전치사 + 목적어

I **looked at** *Johnson*.
I **looked at** *him*.
I **looked** *****Johnson* **at**. (×)
I **looked** *****him* **at**. (×)

제14강 부사

7. 이중부정

단문 속에서는 아래의 표현과 no, not, never를 겹쳐 쓸 수 없다.

---
seldom, hardly, rarely, scarcely, without ~ing

no one, nobody, none, nothing, nowhere

nor V + S, neither V + S

unless S + V

lest S + (should) + 동사원형

She was so tired that she ***couldn't hardly** stay awake. (×)
She was so tired that she **could hardly** stay awake. (○)

비교(Comparison)

1. 원급비교

1) 동등비교

as + 형용사[부사]의 원급 + as ~만큼 …한

He is **as** kind **as** she.
She can swim **as** well **as** you (can).

(cf.) as A as B 형태의 직유 표현
'B처럼 A하다'라는 의미의 관용표현으로, 해석은 '매우 A하다'로 한다.
He is **as busy as a bee**. (몹시 바쁜)
The general was **as brave as a lion**. (매우 용감한)
She is **as cunning as a fox**. (매우 교활한)
He was **as cool as a cucumber** when he get the award. (매우 침착[냉정]한)
The merchant was **as miserable as a fish out of water**. (몹시 비참한)

(cf.) the same + 명사 + as ~와 똑같은
I bought **the same** car **as** yours.

2) 열등비교

not so[as] + 형용사[부사]의 원급 + as ~만큼 …하지 못한

He is **not so[as]** tall **as** his brother.
He is **not so** clever **as** I.
She is **not so** beautiful **as** kind.
= She is **less** beautiful **than** kind.

2. 배수비교

배수사 + as + 원급 + as ~보다도 몇 배 더 …한
= 배수사 + 비교급 + than
= 배수사 + the + 명사 + of

The river is **three times as long as** the Thames.
= The river is **three times longer than** the Thames.
= The river is **three times the length of** the Thames.

(cf.) twice의 경우, 뒤에 '비교급 + than'을 쓸 수 없고 반드시 'as ~ as …'를 써야 한다.
She has **twice** *more money **than** you. (×)
She has **twice as** much money **as** you. (○)

3. 원급비교의 관용표현

1) as + 원급 + as possible 가능한 한 ~하게
 = as + 원급 + as + 주어 + can

I ran **as** fast **as possible**.
= I ran **as** fast **as I could**.

2) as + 원급 + as can be 매우 ~한, 더할 나위 없이 ~한
 = as + 원급 + as anything

He is **as** poor **as (poor) can be**.
Timing is **as** important **as anything**.

3) as + 원급 + as any + 명사 어느 ~에도 못지않게 …한
 = as + 원급 + as ever + 동사

He is **as great as any** statesman in the world.
= He is **as great** a statesman **as ever lived**.
= He is **the greatest statesman** in the world.

4) 부정주어 + so[as]+ 원급 + as 가장 ~한

> **Nothing** is **as** precious **as** health.
> = **Nothing** is **more** precious **than** health.
> = Health is **more** precious **than anything else**.
> = Health is **the most** precious of all.

5) not so much A as B A라기보다는 오히려 B인
   = not A so much as B
   = rather B than A

> He is **not so much** a singer **as** a dancer.
> = He is **not** a singer **so much as** a dancer.
> = He is **rather** a dancer **than** a singer.

6) not so much as ~조차 않다

> He can**not so much as** write his name.

7) as good as ~와 다름없는
   = no better than

> He is **as good as** a beggar.
> = He is **no better than** a beggar.

8) without so much as ~ing ~조차 하지 않고, 심지어 ~조차 없이

> She went out of the school **without so much as saying** a word.
> = She went out of the school **without even saying** a word.

9) as ~ as + 수사 ~씩이나, 무려

> He ate **as** many **as six** apples.
> She played the piano **as** long **as two** hours.

10) as many 같은 수의
    as much 같은 양의

> I waited for ten minutes; it seemed **as many** hours.
> He drank two bottles of beer and **as much** wine.

4. 비교급과 최상급의 형태

1) 단음절어는 어미에 -er, -est를 붙인다.

> Muhammad Ali was one of the **greatest** boxers of all time.

2) -y, -er, -le, -ow 등으로 끝나는 2음절 형용사는 어미에 -er, -est를 붙인다.

happy, heavy, funny, lovely, likely, lively, costly / clever, tender, bitter / able, idle, noble, cruel / narrow, shallow 등

> He is ***more clever** than I. (×)
> He is **cleverer** than I. (○)

(cf.) 형용사에 -ly를 붙여 만든 파생 부사는 2음절어도 more, most를 쓴다.
> You should try to drive ***slowlier**. (×)
> You should try to drive **more slowly**. (○)

3) 그 밖의 대부분의 2음절 및 3음절 이상 단어는 more, most를 쓴다.

> You should be **more careful**.
> Mary's answer is **more correct** than yours.

4) 불규칙 변화

> good/ well - better - best
> bad/ ill - worse - worst
> many/ much - more - most
> little - less - least

5. 의미에 따라 비교급이 달라지는 단어

1) far - farther - farthest (거리)
   far - further - furthest (정도)

   I don't think I can move a step **farther**.
   The issue needs **further** examination.

2) late - later - latest (시간)
   late - latter - last (순서)

   He became Senator two years **later**. (나중에)
   Of the two possibilities, the **latter** seems more likely. (후자)
   My **latest** book created a great sensation. (최근의)
   My **last** plan was successful. (마지막)

3) old - older - oldest (노소·신구)
   old - elder - eldest (형제관계)

   You are much **older** than you look.
   Which of you two is the **elder** brother?

6. 비교급

1) 우등비교: 형용사/부사의 비교급 + than

   He is **taller than** I.
   Soccer is generally **more interesting than** baseball.
   She studies **harder than** her brother.

2) 열등비교: less + 원급 + than

   She is **less** beautiful **than** her sister.
   = She is **not so** beautiful **as** her sister.

7. 동일인·동일물의 성질 비교

동일한 대상의 성질 또는 성향을 비교하는 경우에는 음절수와 무관하게 'more ~ than'의 형태를 사용한다.

My brother is ***cleverer than** honest. (×)
My brother is **more clever than** honest. (○)
= My brother is **rather clever than** honest.
= My brother is **less** honest **than** clever.

8. 라틴어계 형용사의 비교급

라틴어에서 온 형용사의 비교급 뒤에는 than 대신 전치사 to를 사용한다.

superior to ↔ inferior to
senior to ↔ junior to
interior to ↔ exterior to
major to ↔ minor to
prior to ↔ posterior to

He is **superior to** *me* in English.
= He is **better than** *I* in English.
He is five years **senior to** *me*.
= He is **senior to** *me* by five years.
= He is five years **older than** *I*.

9. the + 비교급

1) 'of the two' 혹은 'of A and B' 등의 어구를 동반할 때

Miranda is **the prettier** *of the two*.
Jason is **the taller** *of the two* boys.

(cf.) John is **the tallest** of the three boys. 〈셋 이상일 때는 최상급〉

2) 이유나 원인을 나타내는 절이나 구가 쓰였을 때

I like him **all the better** *because he is honest*.
I like him **all the better** *for his faults*.

3) the + 비교급, the + 비교급 ~하면 할수록 더욱 …하다

The more we have, **the more** we want.
The higher we go up, **the colder** the air becomes.

10. 비교급 관용표현

1) 긍정문 + much[still] more 한층 더[하물며] ~하다
   부정문 + much[still] less 한층 더[하물며] ~않다

He **can** speak French, **much more** English.
She **cannot** speak English, **much less** French.

2) A is no more B than C is D A가 B가 아닌 것은 C가 D가 아닌 것과 같다
   = A is not B any more than C is D
   = A is not B, just as C is not D

A whale is **no more** a fish **than** a horse is.
= A whale is **not** a fish **any more than** a horse is.
= A whale is **not** a fish, **just as** a horse is **not** a fish.

3) A is no less B than C is D C가 D인 것처럼 A는 B이다
   = A is as much B as C is D

A whale is **no less** a mammal **than** a horse is.
= A whale is **as much** a mammal **as** a horse is.

(cf.) She is **no more** beautiful **than** her sister. <둘 다 못생겼다>
She is **not more** beautiful **than** her sister. <언니만큼 예쁘지 않다>
She is **no less** beautiful **than** her sister. <언니와 마찬가지로 예쁘다>
She is **not less** beautiful **than** her sister. <언니 못지않게 예쁘다>

4) know better than to ~할 만큼 어리석지 않다
   = be not so foolish as to

   She **knows better than** to do such a thing.
   = She **is not so foolish as to** do such a thing.

5) no more than = only = as little[few] as 단지, 겨우
   no less than = as many[much] as ~만큼이나
   not more than = at most 기껏해야, 많아야
   not less than = at least 적어도

   He had **no more than** ten dollars.
   He had **not more than** ten dollars.
   He had **no less than** ten dollars.
   He had **not less than** ten dollars.

6) no better than 거의 ~와 같은, ~나 다름없는
   = almost[nearly]

   He is **no better than** a ferocious beast.

7) no longer 더 이상 ~않다
   = not ~ any longer

   I am **no longer** a child.
   = I am **not** a child **any longer**.

8) more than + 수사 ~이상

   This elevator cannot carry **more than** twelve persons.

9) more often than not 자주, 종종
   = as often as not

   More often than not, we take bus to work.

10) more or less 다소; 대체로

> Most people are **more or less** selfish.

11) sooner or later 조만간, 머지않아

> If he continues drinking, **sooner or later** he will lose his job.

12) nothing less than ~와 같은

> It's **nothing less than** madness.

11. 최상급

최상급은 비교대상이 셋 이상인 경우에 쓰며, 일반적으로 정관사 the를 수반한다.

1) the + 최상급 + of all the + 복수명사

> Jack is **the tallest** boy *of all the students*.

2) the + 최상급 + in + 장소

> Jack is **the tallest** boy *in his class*.

3) the + 최상급 + 명사 + (that) ~ ever[can]

> Jack is **the tallest** boy *that has ever lived*.

4) the + 서수 + 최상급

> Jack is **the second tallest** boy in his school.

5) one of the + 최상급 + 복수명사

> Jack is **one of the tallest boys** in his town.

12. 최상급에 정관사 the를 붙이지 않는 경우

1) 동일인·동일물 내에서의 비교

The Pacific ocean is **the deepest** at this point. (×)
The Pacific ocean is **deepest** at this point. (○) 〈태평양 내에서의 비교〉

(cf.) The Pacific ocean is **the largest** in the world. 〈다른 바다와의 비교〉

2) 부사의 최상급

My mother gets up **earliest** in my family.

3) 소유격 뒤

Tom is *John's* **best** friend.

(cf.) (a) most + 형용사/부사(= very)
She is **a most** beautiful student.

13. 최상급 관련 관용표현

> do one's best 최선을 다하다
> make the most[best] of ~을 최대한 이용하다
> at the earliest 빨라도   at first 처음에는
> at least 적어도   at the latest 늦어도
> at (the) most 많아야   at (the) best 기껏해야, 잘 해봐야
> at one's best ~의 전성기에   not in the least 조금도 ~않다
> to say the least 줄잡아 말하더라도   for the most part 대개
> second to none 누구에게도 뒤지지 않는
> the last + 명사 결코 ~할 사람이 아닌

The blooms are **at their best**.
You must **make the best of** your time.
She is **not in the least** interested in the book.
Your performance was **second to none**.
It was informative **for the most part**.
He is **the last man** to break his promise.

14. 비교급과 원급을 이용한 최상급 표현

비교급 + than any other + 단수명사
비교급 + than all the other + 복수명사
비교급 + than anyone[anything] else
비교급 + than any of + 한정사 + 복수명사
부정주어 + 비교급 + than
부정주어 + so + 원급 + as

Miranda is **the brightest student** in the class.
= Miranda is **brighter than any other student** in the class.
= Miranda is **brighter than all the other students** in the class.
= Miranda is **brighter than anyone else** in the class.
= **No other student** in the class is **brighter than** Miranda.
= **No other student** in the class is **so bright as** Miranda.

15. 양보의 의미를 가지는 최상급

The smallest needle will sometimes kill a man.
= Even the smallest needle will sometimes kill a man.
(Even) **The wisest** man does not know everything.

16. 이중비교

원급 비교 뒤에 'if not + 비교급'의 형태가 오는 경우, 다음의 원칙을 따른다.

① 문미에 비교대상이 오면, 접속사 as와 than을 반드시 각각 써 주어야 한다.
② 비교대상이 원급비교의 접속사 as 뒤에 오면, 비교급 뒤에 'than + 비교대상'은 생략한다.

He is **as** rich **as**, if not rich**er than**, *his uncle*.
= He is **as** rich **as** *his uncle*, if not rich**er**.

17. 원급·비교급·최상급을 강조하는 부사

1) very/ quite/ so + 원급

> It is **very foolish** to ask such a thing.
> I see her **quite often**.

2) even/ much/ still/ far/ yet/ a lot + 비교급

> I like red **much better** than pink.
> She earns **a lot more** than I do.

3) much/ by far + the + 최상급
   the very + 최상급

> He is **by far the best** scholar.
> = He is **the very best** scholar.

18. 비교급과 최상급을 쓰지 않는 형용사

절대, 유일의 의미가 내포된 단어들은 원칙적으로 비교급과 최상급을 쓰지 않는다.

absolute, complete, empty, entire, excellent, exquisite, extreme, favorite, full, identical, new, perfect, pregnant, single, square, total, unique, utter, vacant 등

> She's *****the most perfect** candidate for the job. (×)
> She's the **perfect** candidate for the job. (○)

일치(Agreement)

1. 주어와 동사의 수일치

1) 명사 and 명사
단일개념·동일인물을 나타내는 경우는 단수로 취급한다.

*Bread and butte*r **is** my favorite dish. (버터를 바른 빵)
The poet and statesman **is** dead. (시인 겸 정치가)

(cf.) Bread and butter **have** risen in price. (빵과 버터)
The poet and the statesman **are** dead. (시인과 정치가)

2) 상관접속사로 연결된 경우

① **both A and B** A와 B 모두
항상 복수로 취급한다.

Both Jane and Mary **play** the piano.
Both you and he **are** wrong.

② **either A or B** A 또는 B
neither A nor B A도 B도 아닌
not A but B A가 아닌 B
not only A but (also) B A뿐만 아니라 B도
B에 동사를 일치시킨다.

Either you or I **am** in the wrong.
Neither you nor he **is** wrong.
Not only he but also his friends **are** diligent.

③ A as well as B B뿐만 아니라 A도
A에 동사를 일치시킨다.

You as well as he **are** to blame.
The captain as well as the sailors **was** frightened.

3) many + 복수명사 + 복수동사
many a + 단수명사 + 단수동사

Many patients **are** dying.
Many a patient **is** dying.

4) a number of + 복수명사 + 복수동사
the number of + 복수명사 + 단수동사

A number of tickets **are** sold in advance.
The number of tickets **is** limited.

5) 총계·합계 표시어

a series[total/ body/ group/ team] of + 복수명사 + 단수동사

A total of 200 Koreans **lives** in the country.
A series of crimes **has happened** in the village.

6) 부분 표시어

분수/ all/ half/ most/ some/ the rest + of + 한정사 + 단수명사 + 단수동사
분수/ all/ half/ most/ some/ the rest + of + 한정사 + 복수명사 + 복수동사
of 다음에 오는 명사의 수에 동사를 일치시킨다.

Half of my money **is** spent on book.
Half of my books **are** novels.
Two-thirds of the people **are** here.
Two-thirds of the information **is** false.

7) every/ each/ either/ neither + 단수명사 + 단수동사
   each/ either/ neither + of + 한정사 + 복수명사 + 단수동사

> *Each student* **has** his own room.
> *Every train and every steam boat* **was** crowded.
> *Either of the two books* **is** available.
> *Neither of them* **goes** there.

8) more than one[a] + 단수명사 + 단수동사
   more than one of + 한정사 + 복수명사 + 복수동사

> *More than one writer* **has treated** that subject.
> *More than one of the writers* **have treated** that subject.

9) one of + 복수명사 + 단수동사
   the only one of + 복수명사 + 단수동사

> *One of my favorite novels* **is** "Gone with the Wind."
> *The only one of my favorite novels* written in English **is** "Gone with the Wind."

(cf.) one of + 복수명사 + 관계대명사 + 복수동사
   the only one of + 복수명사 + 관계대명사 + 단수동사
   She is one of *my friends* who **understand** me.
   She is *the only one* of my friends who **understands** me.

10) 구와 절 주어

명사구나 명사절이 주어인 경우는 단수로 취급한다.

> *To see* **is** to believe.
> *That she likes children* **is** certain.
> *Who wrote the novels* **is** not known.
> *What I need* **is** money.

11) there is 구문

There is + 단수명사
There are + 복수명사

> There **is** *a table* in the kitchen.
> There **are** *many tables* in the room.

12) 관계사절의 주어와 동사의 수일치

관계사절의 동사는 선행사의 수에 일치시킨다.

> I like *the pencil* that **is** on the desk.
> I like *the pencils* that **are** on the desk.

13) 도치구문에서의 주어와 동사의 수일치

동사 뒤에 위치한 주어와 일치시킨다.

> Blessed **are** *the poor* in spirit.
> So great **was** *her joy* that for the moment she forgot the sad message.
> Beyond the lake and the woods **is** *the house* where my father lives.

14) 단일 개념 주어

기간, 거리, 금액, 무게 등 복수명사가 하나의 단위를 나타낼 때는 단수로 취급한다.

> *Six months* **is** too short a time to learn a language.
> *Twenty miles* **is** a long way to walk.

(cf.) 기간의 경과를 나타내는 경우에는 복수로 취급한다.
> *Ten years* **have passed** since I saw you last.

15) 군집명사 + 복수동사
집합명사 + 단수동사

> *The audience* **were** deeply moved. <군집명사>
> *The audience* **was** not large. <집합명사>

16) 후치수식어를 동반한 주어와 동사의 수일치

> *Ministers* who attended the conference **were** in favor of the plan.
> *The police officer* invited to many schools **seems** very considerate.

2. 대명사 일치

대명사는 선행명사와 성, 수, 인칭이 일치해야 한다.

> *The restaurant* is noted for **its** excellent cuisine.
> *People* often try to emulate **their** favourite movie stars.
> *One* should not do what troubles **one's/ his** conscience.
> *Everyone* may have **his or her** own definition of what love is.

병치(Parallelism)

1. 등위접속사에 의한 병치

1) 명사의 병치

> He is **a teacher, a musician,** *and* ***she writes**. (×)
> He is **a teacher, a musician,** *and* **a writer**. (○)

2) 형용사의 병치

> The crowd was **quiet** *and* ***order** throughout the performance. (×)
> The crowd was **quiet** *and* **orderly** throughout the performance. (○)

3) 부사의 병치

> He finished his work **quickly** *and* ***accurate**. (×)
> He finished his work **quickly** *and* **accurately**. (○)

4) 동사의 병치

> She **got up** early, **ate** breakfast, *and* ***going out** for a walk. (×)
> She **got up** early, **ate** breakfast, *and* **went out** for a walk. (○)

5) 부정사의 병치

He likes **to swim** *and* ***playing*** tennis. (×)
He likes **to swim** *and* **to play** tennis. (○)

(cf.) to부정사가 병치될 때 뒤의 to는 생략할 수 있다.
She usually wants **to read** books, **(to) watch** TV, *or* **(to) go** to the movies.

6) 동명사의 병치

He enjoys **playing** soccer *and* ***to take*** weekend trips. (×)
He enjoys **playing** soccer *and* **taking** weekend trips. (○)

7) 분사의 병치

Surprised *and* ***as she was embarrassed***, she burst into tears. (×)
Surprised *and* **embarrassed**, she burst into tears. (○)

8) 절의 병치

I know **who he is** *and* ***his doings***. (×)
I know **who he is** *and* **what he does**. (○)

(cf.) 종속절의 병치에서 등위접속사 뒤에 오는 절의 접속사는 생략하지 못한다.
We believe **(that) it's a great challenge** *but* ***we can meet that challenge***. (×)
We believe **(that) it's a great challenge** *but* **that we can meet that challenge**. (○)

2. 상관접속사에 의한 병치

다음의 표현에서 A와 B에는 문법적인 구조가 동일한 표현이 와야 한다.

1) both A and B

This book is *both* **interesting** *and* **instructive**.
Investment continues *both* **at home** *and* **in foreign countries**.

2) not only A but also B

> She is *not only* **clever** *but also* **beautiful**.
> The idea is unsound *not only* **in theory** *but also* **in practice**.

3) not A but B

> What he wants to have is *not* **your present** *but* **your mind**.
> She wept *not* **because she was sad** *but* **because she was so pleased**.

4) either A or B

> *Either* **he** *or* **I** am to blame.
> Sightseeing is best done *either* **by tour bus** *or* **by bicycle**.

5) neither A nor B

> She has *neither* **knowledge** *nor* **understanding** of politics.
> It's my principle *neither* **to borrow** *nor* **to lend** money.

3. 비교구문에서의 병치

비교구문에서 비교되고 있는 대상은 그 문법적인 구조와 역할이 서로 같아야 한다.

> **The population of Seoul** is about 3 times as large as ***Busan**. (×)
> **The population of Seoul** is about 3 times as large as **that of Busan**. (○)
> **His salary** is higher than ***John**. (×)
> **His salary** is higher than **John's**. (○)
> She is more popular **in Japan** than ***Korea**. (×)
> She is more popular **in Japan** than **in Korea**. (○)
> **To answer accurately** is more important than ***you finish quickly**. (×)
> **To answer accurately** is more important than **to finish quickly**. (○)

도치(Inversion)

1. 부정 부사·부정 부사구·부정 부사절이 문두에 오는 경우의 도치

at no time, barely, hardly, little, never, no sooner, nor, not only, not until, nowhere, rarely, scarcely, seldom 등

1) be동사: be + S

Rarely **is she** seen in public nowadays.
Not only **was he** driving too fast but he was also thinking of something else.

2) 조동사: 조동사 + S + 동사원형

Nowhere **could we find** the answer to the question.
Under no circumstances **should you lend** him any money.

3) 일반동사: do/ does/ did + S + 동사원형

Little **did I dream** that I should see her there.
Not until I visited her **did I realize** how ill she was.

4) 완료시제 동사: have/ had + S + p.p.

> *Never* **have I seen** her.
> *No sooner* **had he heard** the news than he wept aloud.
> *Hardly* **had he left** home when it began to rain.

2. only가 포함된 부사어가 문두에 오는 경우의 도치

only + 부사어 + 조동사 + 주어 + 동사원형

> *Only after a long argument* **did he agree** to our plan.
> *Only then* **did she know** the seriousness of the situation.
> *Only after he had lost his health* **did he realize** the importance of it.

(cf.) Only, Not only가 주어를 수식하고 있는 경우에는 도치가 일어나지 않는다.
> **Only I** *can do* it.
> **Not only you** but also I *am* to blame.

3. 장소 부사구 뒤의 도치

1형식 문장에서 장소의 부사나 부사구가 문두에 오면, 조동사 없이 '자동사 + 명사 주어'의 순서로 쓴다.

> *At the summit of the mountain* **stood a tall tree**.
> *Among the forests* **was a small cottage**.
> *South of Omaha, Nebraska,* **lies London City**.
> *Here* **comes Mary!**
> *There* **goes your sister!**

(cf.) 주어가 대명사이거나 동사가 타동사인 경우에는 도치가 일어나지 않는다.
> Here ***comes she!*** (×)
> Here **she comes!** (○)
> *On the way there* **we saw** a couple of whales swim right up to our boat.

4. 보어가 강조되어 문두에 오는 경우의 도치

보어 + be동사 + 주어

So old **was the document** that it was barely legible.
Great **was his surprise** when the truth was revealed.
Blessed **are the pure** in heart.

5. 목적어가 부정어를 수반하고 문두에 오는 경우의 도치

Not a word **did she say** all day long.
= She did not say a word all day long.
No mercy **did the cruel king show**.
= The cruel king showed no mercy.

(cf.) 부정어를 동반하지 않은 경우에는 도치가 일어나지 않는다.
　　That promise he broke within a week.
　　What he said I could not understand.

6. as/ than이 쓰인 구문의 도치

비교구문의 접속사 as, than 뒤에서 주어가 명사(구)이고 be동사나 조동사가 쓰인 경우에는 도치가 가능하다.

He earns a lot more *than* **do his friends**.
= He earns a lot more than his friends do.
He traveled widely *as* **did most of his friends**.
= He traveled widely as most of his friends did.

(cf.) 종속절의 주어가 대명사이면 도치시키지 못한다.
　　They arrived earlier *than* *did she. (×)
　　They arrived earlier *than* she did. (○)

7. so/ neither/ nor 구문의 도치

So/ Neither[Nor] + 조동사 + 주어 ~도 역시 마찬가지이다

> He speaks English well. *So* **does his wife**. <긍정문 뒤>
> He does not smoke. *Neither* **does his father**. <부정문 뒤>
> = He does not smoke, *nor* **does his father**.

(cf.) So + S + V 정말 그렇다
  It is raining outside.
  So **it is**. (= Yes it is raining, indeed.)

8. 조건절의 도치

가정법 조건절의 if가 생략되면, had, were, should가 문두로 나가면서 도치가 일어난다.

> **Were I** in your place, I would resign immediately.
> = If I were in your place, I would resign immediately.
> **Had it not been** for your help, I would have failed then.
> = If it had not been for your help, I would have failed then.
> **Should it rain** tomorrow, I shall stay home.
> = If it should rain tomorrow, I shall stay home.

전치사(Preposition)

1. 주요 전치사 비교

1) at/ on/ in

at 시, 분, 정오, 밤 등의 짧은 시각
on 요일, 날짜, 특정일의 아침·오후·저녁 등
in 세기, 년, 월, 계절, 오전, 오후 등

The president is scheduled to speak **at** noon.
I usually go mountain climbing **on** Sunday morning.
I do exercise for half an hour **in** the morning.

2) by/ until[till]

by 어느 때까지의 동작의 완료
until 어느 때까지의 동작의 계속

I want him to finish the work **by** tomorrow.
He will stay here **until(= till)** four o'clock.

3) for/ during

for 수사를 동반하여 일정한 기간을 나타냄
during 기간, 사건의 명사를 동반하여 동작·상태의 계속을 나타냄

He was in a coma **for** three weeks.
During his interview, he answered many questions.

4) since/ from

since '~이래 줄곧'의 뜻으로 과거부터 현재까지의 계속을 표시
from '~로부터'의 뜻으로 till[to]와 함께 쓰여 과거의 출발점만을 표시

I have lived in Seoul **since** my birth.
The dog barked loudly **from** morning *till* night.

5) in/ after

in '~이 지나면'의 뜻으로 주로 미래시제와 함께 쓰임
after '~후에'의 뜻으로 주로 과거시제와 함께 쓰임

She will be discharged from the hospital **in** a week.
Their food supplies gave out **after** a month.

6) on/ beneath

on (표면에 접촉해서) 위에
beneath (표면에 접촉해서) 아래에

There was a picture **on** the wall.
We felt the ground shake **beneath** our feet.

7) above/ below

above (~보다) 위에
below (~보다) 아래에

This mountain is 3,000 meters **above** sea level.
The sun has sunk **below** the horizon.

8) over/ under

over (수직으로) 위에
under (수직으로) 아래에

A lamp was hanging **over** the table.
He fell asleep **under** the tree.

9) between/ among

between (둘) 사이에
among (셋 이상의) 사이에

His house is **between** the school and the park.
The trees were interspersed **among** the houses.

10) by/ beside/ near

by ~의 곁에, 가까이에
beside ~의 옆에 *(cf.)* besides ~외에도
near ~의 근처에, 가까이에 *(cf.)* nearby 가까운

He sat **by** the window and smoked a cigarette.
She rests **beside** her husband in the local cemetery.
There is a park **near** the school.

11) like/ as

like ~처럼
as ~로서

Students were angry at being treated **like** children.
He works **as** a carpenter.

2. 기타 전치사

1) 원인·이유의 전치사

for 감사, 비난, 책임, 유감의 원인
of 병, 굶주림, 노령 등의 내적인 원인
from 피로, 상처, 과로 등의 외적인 원인
through 부주의, 태만, 과오, 결점 등의 간접적 원인

He blamed me **for** the delay.
She died **of** a heart attack.
They died **from** bullet wounds.
He lost his place **through** neglect of duty.

2) 수단·도구의 전치사

with 도구 (~으로, ~을 사용하여)
by 수단, 방법 (~에 의해)
through 수단, 매개 (~을 통하여)

> It is dangerous to play **with** a knife.
> She comes to work **by** bus.
> He spoke **through** an interpreter.

3) 양보의 전치사

in spite of, despite, notwithstanding, for all, with all 등

> He kept on smoking **in spite of** my repeated warning.
> **Despite** the recession, managers decided to raise employee salaries.
> **Notwithstanding** the bad weather, the event was a great success.

4) 예외 표시의 전치사

but, except, except for, with the exception of 등

> No one **but** him knew what to do.
> The shop is open **except** Sunday.
> **Except for** math, his grades were not good.

5) 관련의 전치사

about, as regards, as to, concerning, regarding, in[with] regard to, in[with] respect to 등

> He wrote a book **about** the origin of the universe.
> There are many theories **concerning** the cause of the Great Depression.
> **With regard to** this matter, we will talk with you later.

3. 주요 전치사구

according to ~에 따라서, ~에 의하면
apart from ~은 별문제로 하고, ~은 제쳐두고
as a result of ~의 결과로
at the cost[expense] of ~을 희생하여
at the mercy of ~에 좌우되어, ~의 처분대로
by means[dint/ virtue] of ~의 덕택으로, ~에 의해서
by way of ~을 경유하여; ~하기 위하여
for the purpose of ~할 목적으로
for the sake of ~을 위하여
in accordance with ~에 따라서, ~와 일치하여
in addition to ~이외에도, ~뿐만 아니라
in behalf of ~을 위하여
in case of ~의 경우에는
in comparison with ~과 비교하면
in favor of ~에 찬성하여; ~을 위하여
in honor of ~에 경의를 표하여, ~을 축하하여
in proportion to ~에 비례하여
in pursuit of ~을 찾아서, ~을 추구하여
in response to ~에 응하여[답하여]
instead of ~대신에
in terms of ~의 면에서, ~의 관점에서
in the course of ~하는 동안에
irrespective of ~와 상관없이, ~을 고려하지 않고
on behalf of ~을 대표하여; ~을 위하여
on the basis of ~을 기준으로 하여, ~에 기초하여
thanks to ~덕분에, ~때문에

The ship was **at the mercy of** the wind and waves.
I went to London **by way of** Paris.
Our organization was founded **for the sake of** charity.
She acted **in accordance with** her words.
He rides the clutch **in case of** accidents.

4. 전치사에 따라 뜻이 달라지는 표현

1) agree with + 사람 ~와 의견이 일치하다
   agree to[on] + 사물 ~에 동의하다

   > I **agree with** you in all your views.
   > They all **agreed to** all offer.

2) be concerned about ~을 걱정하다
   be concerned with ~에 관계가 있다

   > We **are concerned about** his financial situation.
   > Her job **is** mainly **concerned with** sales and promotion.

3) be made of ~으로 만들어지다 (물리적 변화)
   be made from ~으로 만들어지다 (화학적 변화)

   > Cloth **is made of** cotton, silk, wool and nylon.
   > Wine **is made from** grapes.

4) call on + 사람 방문하다
   call at + 장소 (장소에) 들르다
   call for 요구하다

   > I'd like to **call on** you tomorrow afternoon.
   > I will **call at** your house tomorrow.
   > They have **called for** an end to violence.

5) compare A with B A와 B를 비교하다
   compare A to B A를 B에 비유하다

   > We **compared** the translation **with** the original.
   > Some people have **compared** books **to** friends.

6) consist of ~으로 구성되다
    consist in ~에 있다

    A molecule of water **consists of** two atoms of hydrogen and one atom of oxygen.
    True education does not **consist in** simply being taught facts.

7) differ from ~와 다르다
    differ in ~에 있어서 다르다

    Plants **differ from** animals because they use photosynthesis.
    The two countries **differ in** religion and culture.

8) result in ~을 초래하다
    result from ~에서 기인하다

    Bad data can **result in** bad decisions.
    Tooth decay can **result from** poor care of your teeth.

9) succeed in 성공하다
    succeed to 계승하다

    He **succeeded in** discovery.
    He **succeeded to** the throne.

10) wait for 기다리다
    wait on 시중들다

    She **waited for** her father all night long.
    The waitress **waited on** him in the restaurant.

5. 전치사의 생략

1) 시간, 거리, 방법, 정도의 명사

> He walked **(for) ten miles**.
> There is no reason for you to act **(in) that way**.

2) 나이, 크기, 색깔, 가격, 모양 등의 명사

> We are **(of) the same age**.
> This book is **(of) the same size** as that.

3) last/ next/ this/ that/ every + 시간명사

> There was a bad storm **last week**.
> I used to stay at home on the loaf **every Sunday**.

특수구문
(Particular Sentence)

1. 부가의문문

주절이 긍정이면 부정의 부가의문문을, 부정이면 긍정의 부가의문문을 쓴다.

1) 주절에 be동사가 있으면 be동사로, 조동사가 있으면 조동사로, 일반동사가 있으면 do[does/ did]동사로 쓴다.

> You *are* really interested in Korean music, **aren't you**?
> He *won't* attend today's meeting, **will he**?
> She *plays* the piano well, **doesn't she**?

(cf.) have가 본동사로 사용되면 부가의문문을 do[does/ did]동사로, 조동사로 사용되면 have[has/ had]동사로 쓴다.
  Tom *has* a book, **doesn't he**? 〈본동사〉
  You *have been* to Busan, **haven't you**? 〈조동사〉

2) 명령문의 부가의문문

주절이 긍정이든 부정이든 부가의문문은 언제나 'will you?'를 쓰며, 권유의 뜻으로 쓰인 명령문은 'won't you?'를 쓴다. Let's로 시작되는 권유문의 경우 부가의문문은 'shall we?'를 쓴다.

> Open the window, **will you**?
> Don't forget this advice, **will you**?
> Have a cup of coffee, **won't you**?
> Let's go shopping together, **shall we**?

3) 주절에 never, no, nothing, hardly, scarcely, seldom 등의 부정어가 있을 경우, 부가의문문은 긍정으로 쓴다.

> We have *no* time to lose, **do we**?
> She *seldom* makes any mistake, **does she**?

4) have to/ had to는 don't, didn't, should/ ought to는 shouldn't, had better는 hadn't, used to는 didn't를 쓴다.

> You *have to* study English, **don't you**?
> I *ought to* go by plane, **shouldn't I**?
> You *had better* go at once, **hadn't you**?
> You *used to* read by the hour, **didn't you**?

5) There로 시작하는 유도부사 구문의 부가의문문은 그대로 there를 쓴다.

> *There was* a large attendance at the theater, **wasn't there**?

6) 지시대명사 This/ That의 부가의문문은 it, These/ Those의 부가의문문은 they를 쓴다.

> *That's* your house, **isn't it**?
> *These* are their houses, **aren't they**?

7) 'I think[believe/ guess/ imagine/ suppose] + that절'의 경우는 that절의 주어와 동사에 맞춰 부가의문문을 만든다. 단, 주절이 부정이면 부가의문문은 긍정으로 쓴다.

> I think that you *will make* it, **won't you**?
> I *don't* suppose that she *will come*, **will she**?

2. It is ~ that … 강조구문

강조하는 어구가 It is와 that 사이에 온다.

1) 단어의 강조시에는 that 대신 강조어구에 따라 who(사람), which(사물) 등을 쓸 수 있다.

> I broke the window yesterday.
> → **It was** *I* **that[who]** broke the window yesterday.
> → **It was** *the window* **that[which]** I broke yesterday.
> → **It was** *yesterday* **that[when]** I broke the window.

2) 부사구(절)의 강조시에는 that만 쓸 수 있다.

> **It was** *with these words* **that** he concluded his speech.

3) 의문사 강조

> What do you want to say?
> → *What* **is it that** you want to say?
> Who has played such a trick on you?
> → *Who* **is it that** has played such a trick on you?

4) It ~ that 강조구문과 가주어-진주어 구문의 구별

강조장치(It is ~ that)을 제외한 나머지 부분만으로 완전한 문장이 되면 강조구문이고, 그렇지 않으면 가주어-진주어 구문이다.

> **It is** you **that[who]** are to blame for the accident. <강조구문>
> **It is** natural **that** parents should love their children. <가주어-진주어 구문>

3. 생략

1) 반복을 피하기 위한 생략

> The girl got hurt, and **(she)** went to hospital.
> Some people go to the mountain, and others **(go)** to the seaside.
> To some life is pleasure; to others **(life is)** suffering.
> You may read this book if you want to **(read this book)**.
> I like you better than he **(likes you)**.
> Will it rain tomorrow? — I hope **(that it will)** not **(rain)**.

2) 부사절에서 '주어 + be동사'의 생략

when, while, if, though, as 등이 이끄는 부사절의 주어가 주절의 주어와 같은 경우

When **(she was)** young, she had a keen interest in writing.
He collapsed with a heart attack *while* **(he was)** exercising.

3) 관용적인 생략

인사말, 감사, 권유, 속담, 게시문 등

(I wish you a) Happy New Year!
(I wish you) Have a good day.
(I) Thank you so much.
The sooner **(you do it)**, the better **(it will be)**.
(If one is) Out of sight, **(one is)** out of mind.
No smoking (is allowed here).
(The store is) Closed today.
(Keep your) Hands off.

4. 동격

명사상당어구를 이용하여 앞에 나온 말을 구체적으로 설명한다.

1) 명사

Mr. Smith, **a psychiatrist**, solved her mental problems.
Thomas Edison, **an American inventor**, invented the light bulb.

2) 동격의 of

She was deeply saddened by *the news* **of her friend's death**.
He gave up *the idea* **of borrowing money**.

3) 부정사

He has but *one aim* in life, **to make money**.
I made *a decision* **to go abroad to study English**.

4) 명사절

> The actress hid *the fact* **that she was married**.
> I have no *idea* **how long he has been in office**.
> *The question* arose **who was to receive him**.

5. 삽입

부가적으로 설명하기 위한 단어, 구, 절 등을 문장에 끼워 넣을 수 있다.

1) 단어의 삽입

> He had, **surprisingly**, paid for everything.
> Even a small pet, **however**, can be a lot of work.

2) 구의 삽입

> He was, **so to speak**, an outsider.
> We were, **believe it or not**, in love with each other.

3) 절의 삽입

> His idea, **it seems to me**, is the best.
> I voted for a person who **I think** is qualified for the job.
> The judge, **who was honest**, was respected by all the people.
> The company, **(which was) founded in 1932**, is based in New York.
> She is, **as I said before**, a charming young woman.

4) 관용적인 삽입절

few[little], if any, + 명사 ~이 있다 하더라도 거의 없다
seldom[rarely], if ever, + 동사 ~하는 일이 있다 하더라도 드물다

> There are *few*, **if any**, *errors*.
> She *seldom*, **if ever**, *goes* to the theatre.

MEMO

MEMO

MEMO